on
melancholy

Published by Hesperus Press Limited
28 Mortimer Street, London W1W 7RD
www.hesperuspress.com

First published by Hesperus Press Limited, 2013

Introduction © Nicholas Robins, 2013

Selection © Hesperus Press, 2013

Extracts from Robert Burton's *The Anatomy of Melancholy*, by Floyd Dell
and Paul Jordan-Smith (eds.), published by Farrar and Rinehart (1927).
Every effort has been made to obtain permission from copyright holders to
reproduce this material. Owing to the age of the text, and given the resources
available to the publisher, this has not been possible. Any queries relating
to copyright in this book should be referred to the publisher for immediate
attention.

Designed and typeset by Fraser Muggeridge studio

Printed and bound by CPI Group (UK) Ltd, Croydon, CR0 4YY

ISBN: 978-1-84391-6-222

Burton
on
melancholy

Edited by Nicholas Robins

'on'

Contents

Introduction

Exuberant, copious, colloquial and chaotic; crammed with arcane erudition and interrupted by intemperate satire and playful exaggeration, *The Anatomy of Melancholy*, the masterpiece of a seventeenth-century Oxford don, was a popular success on its first appearance in 1621. In the eighteenth century it was borrowed by Laurence Sterne in *Tristram Shandy* and was the only book that got Dr Johnson 'out of bed two hours sooner than he wished to rise'.* After it resurfaced in 1798, Keats drew on it for his narrative poem 'Lamia' and his 'Ode on Melancholy'; Coleridge greatly admired it, Charles Lamb imitated its style and Byron viewed it as a capacious hold-all of entertainingly obscure scholarship, invaluable to anyone who wished 'to acquire a reputation of being well read with the least trouble'.† It flavours the melancholy comedy of Anthony Powell and amused Anthony Burgess. It taught V.S. Pritchett's atheistic uncle to read and armed him with a secular Bible with which to combat his hymn-singing, chapel-going relatives.‡ And in 1997, a visit to the memorials of its author in Oxford brings a moment of quiet, ironic happiness to the flâneurs in Patrick Keiller's psychogeographical film, *Robinson in Space*.

Who was Robert Burton? The surviving facts are few. He was born in 1577 near Nuneaton in Leicestershire, the younger son of an ancient, unremarkable, gentry family, educated at Brasenose College, Oxford, and moved to Christ Church as a Student (or Fellow) in 1599. He sought ecclesiastical preferment, but failed to get it, and seems to have resigned himself to a quiet academic life. For three years he was a clerk of the Oxford market, responsible for regulating dealings between the University and the city

* James Boswell, *Life of Johnson*, 1791
† Byron, *Letters*, 1807
‡ V.S. Pritchett, *A Cab at the Door*, 1968

traders; later (much more his style) he was appointed Librarian at Christ Church. He was granted church livings in Oxford, Lincolnshire and near the family home in Leicestershire, where most of his duties would have been discharged by curates. He seems not to have consorted with fellow churchmen and he resisted the temptation to add his mote to that century's growing heap of theological books (as he might have been expected to do). He wrote some poems and one complete play, *Philosophaster*, an academic Jonsonian satire. Perhaps he would have preferred to live as some kind of freelance writer, but his failure to gain much from any patron, and his attachment to Christ Church, 'the most flourishing College of Europe' as he called it, suggest that the relatively secure existence of an academic bachelor – 'a silent, sedentary, solitary, private life' – suited him better. (Although Christ Church in the late 1620s was, in fact, riven by constitutional controversy, and at one point Burton considered leaving Oxford.) The rumour put about after his death in 1640 that he had hanged himself is unfounded: he would not otherwise have been buried in the cathedral at Christ Church. More intriguing is the gap in his life story in the later 1590s. Was he himself afflicted? Was he down in the dumps? Was he, in fact, the same 20-year-old Robert Burton who in 1597 consulted the doctor, astrologer and therapist Simon Forman, complaining of 'melancholy'? The dates fit.

And it would be fitting, since the 'heavy heart' he complains of and the measures he took to cure it – that is, the writing of the *Anatomy* itself – were the major events of his life. For the primary reason, or at least the pretext, he gives us for composing his book was 'by being busy to avoid melancholy': the *Anatomy* was a vast self-help project to cure the malady in himself, and a manual to cure or at least ameliorate it in others. Like Montaigne, he took himself as a starting-point for his enquiry. But beyond this, the author had a more ambitious purpose – and this was to reform society. For Burton, though hardly straying from a few English counties – never travelling 'but in

Map or Card' – was dismayed and disgusted at what he knew about the world. Contemporary Europe was racked by civil war, religious strife and superstition; England mired in sloth, injustice, corruption and wasted opportunities – and the cause of these, Burton believed, was melancholy. Mankind was too irrational to be reasoned into a better way of organising its affairs. What was called for was nothing less than a change in the psychological basis of mankind. Cure melancholy, and you might surely make some progress against the social inertia and chaos of contemporary society, towards something resembling the benign and reasonable utopia Burton describes in the opening pages of the *Anatomy*. And this is one reason why Burton's melancholy includes not merely what we might describe as 'depression', but the whole 'melancholy madness' of mankind and made of his book an *omnium gatherum* of the ills of the world.

This is also why Burton takes little interest in the familiar idea, begun by Aristotle and later refined and elevated in the Renaissance by Marsilio Ficino, that melancholy could lend its objects intellectual and spiritual prestige or that it was the badge of genius. There is no sense in the *Anatomy* that anyone might wish to cultivate melancholy or adopt it as an artistic pose. For Burton, it was a degenerate state, and his object was to collect and summarise everything significant written on the subject since antiquity; to describe, as his elaborate title page declares 'what it is, with all its kinds, causes, symptoms, prognostics and several cures'. The scientific foundation of this exploration was the ancient theory of the four humours – sanguine, phlegmatic, choleric and melancholic – and in particular the idea of 'melancholy adust', the condition which arose from the burning or corrupting of any person's dominant humour. His method was to examine hundreds of literary examples, separating, dividing and dissecting them (like an anatomist) and observing parallels, qualifications and contradictions to arrive at some kind of truth. The persona he adopted in this pursuit – at least in the opening section of the *Anatomy* – is that of Democritus, the 'laughing philosopher', who, when visited by Hippocrates, was found dissecting animals to discover the source of 'black bile', the seat of melancholy. The result was a vast summation of the received wisdom of centuries of writing on morbid psychology, and an English encyclopedia to rival contemporary achievements on the continent.

Fortunately, it is a good deal more and less than any modern notion of an encyclopedia, with all the familiar qualities of impersonality, rigorous organisation, strict editorial control – and eventual obsolescence. For, like its own subject, the *Anatomy* is a great 'stupend', a gallimaufry of different moods, styles, subjects, digressions and contradictions. There may be method in the madness – following his long address to the reader (a book in itself) Burton divided his work into three main 'partitions', dealing in the first with the causes of melancholy, the second with its cures and the third with the special problems of love and religious melancholy – but most readers of the whole work, wonderingly following Burton on one of his extended digressions on spirits, fossils, foreign travel or astronomy must sometimes question whether the author had complete control over his material and often struggle to keep his submerged logic in view. Is he leading himself and his readers into a Serbonian Bog of his own making? Looking at the elaborate synopses created for each partition, it's sometimes difficult to resist the suspicion that there was a touch of insanity in Burton's approach, complicated by the huge additions he made to subsequent editions of his work.

But there is nothing insane about the voice that carries us through his long journey – nothing saner or more reasonable; more personable or personal. Burton's prose is especially lively than when his subject leads him into some personal domain – the tyranny of a grammar school education, the miseries of scholars, the pains of disappointed preferment – or (and they sometimes overlap) when he has one of his pet hates in sight – the English gentry (stingy, philistine, lazy, superficial), the Catholic Church (bullying, grasping, dishonest), Islam (cruel, superstitious, ridiculous). In these passages, Burton often seems at his most modern, liberal and humane. The overall impression is Janus-faced, or, as the Burton scholar Michael O'Connell* has pointed out, of two books coexisting in one:

One is the complete medical treatise on melancholy, an 'anatomy' properly speaking. The other is a work of humanist wisdom, a kind of commentary on human nature and, implicitly, on human knowing.

There is a very long history of abridging and of extracting material from *The Anatomy of Melancholy* and the book is so long and various that any number of different selections might have been made which would hardly repeat the same material. On the whole I have shied away from Burton's supernatural divagations or the more technical and medical passages, and picked those in which he seems most emotionally engaged. The selection is taken from the edition edited by Floyd Dell and Paul Jordan-Smith in 1927, the only one to replace the author's huge quantity of Latin quotations with English translations. Burton – who was only discouraged by his publishers from writing the whole of the *Anatomy* in Latin – would have deplored this innovation, but I make no apology for choosing their version. The greatest problem for most readers presented with a copy of the original text is the frequent Latin citation, even when Burton, as he often does, follows these with an approximate translation or paraphrase. The translated passages are rendered here in italics.

The best modern editions of the full text are published by the New York Review of Books, edited in one volume by Holbrook Jackson, and the magnificent six-volume edition published by Oxford University Press.

– Nicholas Robins, 2013

* Michael O'Connell, *Robert Burton*, 1986; quoted in J.B. Bamborough's introduction to the first volume of the Oxford University Press edition of *The Anatomy of Melancholy*, 1989

On melancholy

Democritus Junior to the Reader

Burton addresses the reader in the guise of a latter-day Democritus, the 'laughing philosopher' of ancient Greece.

Gentle reader, I presume thou wilt be very inquisitive to know what antick or personate actor this is that so insolently intrudes upon this common theatre to the world's view, arrogating another man's name; whence he is, why he doth it, and what he hath to say. Although, as [Seneca] said, *In the first place, supposing I do not wish to answer, who shall make me?* I am a free man born, and may choose whether I will tell; who can compel me? If I be urged, I will as readily reply as that Egyptian in Plutarch, when a curious fellow would needs know what he had in his basket, *When you see the cover, why ask about the thing hidden?* It was therefore covered, because he should not know what was in it. Seek not after that which is hid; if the contents please thee, and be for thy use, suppose the Man in the Moon, or whom thou wilt to be the Author; I would not willingly be known. Yet in some sort to give thee satisfaction, which is more than I need [do], I will shew a reason, both of this usurped name, title and subject. And first of the name of *Democritus*; lest any man by reason of it should be deceived, expecting a pasquil, a satire, some ridiculous treatise (as I myself should have done), some prodigious tenent*, or paradox of the Earth's motion, of infinite Worlds in an infinite waste, so caused by an accidental collision of Motes in the Sun, all which Democritus held, Epicurus and their Master Leucippus of old maintained, and are lately revived by Copernicus, Brunus, and some others. Besides, it hath been always an ordinary custom, as Gellius observes, for later writers and imposters to broach many absurd and insolent fictions under

* Tenet

the name of so noble a philosopher as Democritus, to get themselves credit and by that means the more to be respected; as artificers usually do, ascribing a new statue to Praxitiles himself. 'Tis not so with me.

No Centaurs here, or Gorgons look to find,
My subject is of man, and human kind.
– Martial

Thou thyself art the subject of my discourse.

Democritus Senior

Democritus, as he is described by Hippocrates and Laertius, was a little wearish old man, very melancholy by nature, averse from company in his latter days, and much given to solitariness, a famous Philosopher in his age, coeval with Socrates, wholly addicted to his studies at the last, and to a private life: writ many excellent works, a great Divine, according to the divinity of those times, as an expert Physician, a Politician, an excellent Mathematician, Diacosmus and the rest of his works do witness. [...] After a wandering life he settled at Abdera, a town in Thrace, and was sent for thither to be their Lawmaker, Recorder, or Town Clerk, as some will; or as others, he was there bred and born. Howsoever it was, there he lived at last in a garden in the suburbs, wholly betaking himself to his studies and a private life, saving that sometimes he would walk down to the haven, and laugh heartily at such variety of ridiculous objects, which there he saw. Such a one was Democritus.

Burton's self-description

But in the mean time, how doth this concern me, or upon what reference do I usurp his habit? I confess indeed that to compare myself unto him for ought I have yet said, were both impudency and arrogancy: I do not presume to make any parallel; he outranks me by countless numbers; I am inconsiderable, nothing at all; I do not aspire to greatness, nor hope for it. Yet this much I will say of myself, and that I hope without all suspicion of pride, or self-conceit, I have lived a silent, sedentary, solitary, private life, with myself and the Muses in the University as long almost as Xenocrates in Athens, nearly to old age, to learn wisdom as he did, penned up most part in my study. For I have been brought up a student in the most flourishing College of Europe, the most august College*, and can brag with Jovius, almost, *in that splendour of Vaticanish retirement, confined to the company of the distinguished, I have spent thirty-seven full and fortunate years*; for thirty years I have continued (having the use of as good Libraries as ever he had) a scholar, and would be therefore loth, either by living as a drone, to be an unprofitable or unworthy Member of so learned and noble a society, or to write that which should be any way dishonourable to such a royal and ample foundation. Something I have done, though by my profession a Divine, yet *being carried away by a giddy disposition*, as he [Scaliger] said, out of a running wit, an unconstant, unsettled mind, I had a great desire (not able to attain superficial skill in any) to have some smattering in all, to be Somebody in everything, Nothing in anything, which Plato commends, out of him Lipsius approves and furthers, *as fit to be imprinted in all curious wits, not to be a slave of one science, or dwell altogether in one subject, as most do, but to rove abroad*, the servant of a hundred arts, *to have an oar in every man's boat, to taste of every dish, and sip of every cup*, which saith Montaigne, was well performed by Aristotle, and his learned countryman Adrian Turnebus. This roving humour, (though not with like success) I have ever had, and like a ranging spaniel, that barks at every bird he sees, leaving his game, I have followed all, saving that which I should, and may justly complain, and truly (for who is everywhere is nowhere), which Gesner did in modesty, that I have read many books, but to little purpose, for want of good method; I have confusedly tumbled over divers authors in our Libraries,

* Christ Church, Oxford

with small profit, for want of art, order, memory, judgement. I never travelled but in Map or Card, in which my unconfined thoughts have freely expatiated, as having ever been especially delighted with the study of Cosmography. Saturn was the Lord of my geniture, culminating, etc., and Mars principal significator* of manners in partile† conjunction with mine Ascendant; both fortunate in their houses, etc.. I am not poor, I am not rich, nothing's here, but nothing's lacking, I have little, I want nothing; all my treasure is in Minerva's tower. Greater preferment, as I could never get, so I am not in debt for it; I have a competency (praise God) from my noble and munificent Patrons, though I live still a Collegiate student, as Democritus in his garden, and lead a monastic life, a theatre to myself, sequestered from those tumults and troubles of the world, as he [Heinsius] said, and in some high place above you all, like the wise Stoick, seeing all ages, past and present, as at one glance: I hear and see what is done abroad, how others run, ride, turmoil and macerate themselves in court and country; far from those wrangling lawsuits, courts of vanity, marts of ambition, I am wont to laugh with myself: I laugh at all, [each] *only secure lest my suit go amiss, my shops perish*, corn and cattle miscarry, trade decay. *I have no wife nor children, good or bad, to provide for.* A mere spectator of other men's fortunes and adventures, and how they act their parts, which methinks are diversely presented unto me, as from a common theatre or scene. I hear new news every day, and those ordinary rumours of war, plagues, fires, inundations, thefts, murders, massacres, meteors, comets, spectrums, prodigies, apparitions, of towns taken, cities besieged in France, Germany, Turkey, Persia, Poland, etc., daily musters and preparations, and such like, which these tempestuous times afford, battles fought, so many men slain, monomachies‡, shipwrecks, piracies, and sea-

* Ruler

† Exact

‡ Contests

fights, peace, leagues, stratagems, and fresh alarms. A vast confusion of vows, wishes, actions, edicts, petitions, lawsuits, pleas, laws, proclamations, complaints, grievances, are daily brought to our ears. New books every day, pamphlets, currantoes*, stories, whole catalogues of volumes of all sorts, new paradoxes, opinions, schisms, heresies, controversies in philosophy, religion, etc.. Now come tidings of weddings, maskings, mummeries, entertainments, jubilees, embassies, tilts and tournaments, trophies, triumphs, revels, sports, plays: then again, as in a new shifted scene, treasons, cheating tricks, robberies, enormous villainies in all kinds, funerals, burials, deaths of Princes, new discoveries, expeditions; now comical then tragical matters. Today we hear of new Lords and officers created, tomorrow of some great men deposed, and then again of fresh honours conferred; one is let loose, another imprisoned; one purchaseth, another breaketh; he thrives, his neighbour turns bankrupt; now plenty, then again dearth and famine; one runs, another rides, wrangles, laughs, weeps etc.. Thus I daily hear, and such like, both private and publick news. Amidst the gallantry and misery of the world; jollity, pride, perplexities and cares, simplicity and villainy; subtlety, knavery, candour and integrity, mutually mixed and offering themselves, I rub on in a strictly private life; as I have still lived, so I now continue, as I was from the first, left to a solitary life, and mine own domestick discontents: saving that sometimes, not to tell a lie, as Diogenes went into the city, and Democritus to the haven, to see fashions, I did for my recreation now and then walk abroad, look into the world, and could not choose but make some little observation, not so wise an observer as a plain rehearser, not as they did to scoff or laugh at all, but with a mixed passion.

Burton gives his reasons for writing

If any man except against the matter or manner of treating of this subject, and will demand a reason of it, I can allege more than

* Newsletters

one. I writ of melancholy, by being busy to avoid melancholy. There is no greater cause of melancholy than idleness, no better cure than business, as Rhasis holds: and howbeit to be busied in toys is to small purpose, yet hear that divine Seneca: Better do to no end than nothing. I writ therefore, and busied myself in this playing labour that I might avoid the torpor of laziness, with Vectius in Macrobius, and turn my leisure to purpose. [...] I might be of Thucydides' opinion: To know a thing and not express it, is all one as if he knew it not. When I first took this task in hand, and as he saith, undertook the work, my genius impelling me, this I aimed at: to ease my mind by writing, for I had a heavy heart and an ugly head, a kind of imposthume in my head, which I was very desirous to be unladen of, and could imagine no fitter evacuation than this. Besides I might not well refrain, for one must needs scratch where it itches. I was not a little offended with this malady, shall I say my Mistress Melancholy, my Egeria, or my Evil Genius? And for that cause, as he that is stung with a scorpion, I would expel one nail with another, idleness with idleness, the antidote from the Viper, make an Antidote out of that which was the prime cause of my disease. [...]

I would help others out of a fellow-feeling, and as that virtuous Lady did of old, being a Leper herself, bestow all her portion to build an Hospital for Lepers, I will spend my time and knowledge, which are my greatest fortunes, for the common good of all.

The itch to write

'Tis most true that many are possessed by an incurable itch to write, and there is no end of writing of books, as the Wise-man found of old, in this scribbling age especially, wherein the number of books is without number (as a worthy man saith), presses be oppressed, and out of an itching humour, that every man hath to show himself, desirous of fame and honour (we all write, learned and unlearned) he will write no matter what, and scrape together it boots not whence. [...] As Apothecaries we make new mixtures every day, pour out of one vessel into another; and as those old

Romans robbed all the cities of the world, to set out their bad-sited Rome, we skim off the cream of other men's wits, pick the choice flowers of their tilled gardens to set out our own sterile plots. They lard their lean books (so Jovius inveighs) with the fat of others' works, the blundering thieves. A fault that every Writer finds, as I do now, and yet faulty themselves. *Men of three letters*, all thieves; they pilfer out of old Writers to stuff up their new Comments, scrape Ennius' dung-hills, and out of Democritus' pit, as I have done. By which means it comes to pass, that not only libraries and shops are full of our putrid papers, but that every close-stool and jakes are well supplied with privy-poetry; they serve to put under pies, to lap spice in, and keep roast-meat from burning. With us in France, saith Scaliger, every man hath liberty to write, but few ability. Heretofore learning was graced by judicious scholars, but now noble sciences are vilified by base and illiterate scribblers, that either write for vain-glory, need, to get money, or as Parasites to flatter and collogue* with some great men, they put out trifles, rubbish and trash. [...] What a catalogue of new books all this year, all this age (I say) have our Frankfurt Marts, our domestick Marts, brought out! Twice a year we stretch our wits out, and set them to sale; after great toil we attain nothing. So that, which Gesner much desires, if a speedy reformation be not had, by some Princes' Edicts and grave Supervisors, to restrain this liberty, it will run on to infinity. What a glut of books! Who can read them? As already, we shall have a vast Chaos and confusion of Books, we are oppressed with them, our eyes ache with reading, our fingers with turning. For my part I am one of the number – one of the many – I do not deny it; I have only this of Macrobius to say for myself, *'tis all mine and none mine.*

> *As bees in flowery glades sip every plant*
> *Lucretius*

* Consult, confer

As a good housewife out of divers fleeces weaves one piece of cloth, a bee gathers wax and honey out of many flowers, and makes a new bundle of all, I have laboriously collected this Cento* out of divers Writers, and that without injury, I have wronged no authors, but given every man his own. [...] And for those other faults of barbarism, Dorick† dialect, extemporanean style, tautologies, apish imitation, a rhapsody of rags gathered together from several dung-hills, excrements of authors, toys and fopperies confusedly tumbled out, without art, invention, judgement, wit, learning, harsh, raw, rude, phantastical, absurd, insolent, indiscreet, ill-composed, indigested, vain, scurrile, idle, dull and dry, I confess all ('tis partly affected), thou canst not think worse of me than I do of myself. 'Tis not worth the reading, I yield it, I desire thee not to lose time in perusing so vain a subject, I should be peradventure loth myself to read him or thee so writing, 'tis not worth while.

A loose, plain, rude writer
I have no such skill to make new men at my pleasure, or means to hire them, no whistle to call like the master of a ship, and bid them run etc.. I have no such authority, no such benefactors, as that noble Ambrosius was to Origen, allowing him six or seven amanuenses to write out his dictates; I must for that cause do my business myself and was therefore enforced, as a bear doth her whelps, to bring forth this confused lump, I had not time to lick it into form, as she doth her young ones, but even so to publish it, as it was first written, whatever came uppermost, in an extemporean style, as I do commonly all other exercises; I put forth what my genius dictated, out of a confused company of notes, and writ with as small deliberation as I do ordinarily speak, without all affectation of big words, fustian phrases, jingling terms, tropes, strong lines, that like

* A literary patchwork pieced together from other works
† Rustic

Acestes' arrows caught fire as they flew, strains of wit, brave heats, elogies, hyperbolical exornations*, elegancies, etc., which many so much affect. I am a water-drinker, drink no wine at all, which so much improves our modern wits, a loose, plain, rude writer, and as free as loose, I call a spade a spade, I write for minds not ears, I respect matter, not words; remembering that of Cardan, Words exist for things, not things for words. [...] 'Tis not my study or intent to compose neatly, which an Orator requires, but to express myself readily and plainly as it happens. So that as a River runs, sometimes precipitate and swift, then dull and slow; now direct, then winding; now deep, then shallow; now muddy, then clear; now broad, then narrow; doth my style flow: now serious, then light; now comical, then satirical; now more elaborate, then remiss, as the present subject required, or as at that time I was affected. And if thou vouchsafe to read this treatise, it shall seem no otherwise to thee than the way to an ordinary Traveller, sometimes fair, sometimes foul; here champaign, there inclosed; barren in one place, better soil in another; by woods, groves, hills, dales, plains, etc. I shall lead thee over steep mountains, through treacherous valleys, dew-clad meadows and rough plowed fields, through variety of objects, that which thou shalt like and surely dislike.

Humanity remains the same

'Tis not to be denied, the world alters every day, cities fall, kingdoms are transferred; as Petrarch observes: We change language, habits, laws, customs, manners, but not vices, not diseases, not the symptoms of folly and madness – they are still the same. And as a river, we see, keeps the like name and place, but not water, and yet ever runs, our times and persons alter, vices are the same, and ever will be. Look how nightingales sang of old, cocks crowed, kine lowed, sheep bleated, sparrows chirped, dogs barked, so they do still; we keep our madness still, play the fools still, the play's

* Embellishments

not finished yet, we are of the same humours and inclinations as our predecessors were, you shall find us all alike, much at one, we and our sons, and so shall our posterity continue to the last.

The mischief of great men

Of fifteen thousand proletaries* slain in a battle, scarce fifteen are recorded in history, or one alone, the General perhaps, and after a while his and their names are likewise blotted out, the whole battle itself is forgotten. Those Grecian orators, with the greatest force of genius and eloquence, set out the renowned overthrows at Thermopylae, Salamis, Marathon, Mycale, Mantinea, Chaeronea, Plataea. The Romans record their battle at Cannae, and Pharsalian fields, but they do but record, and we scarce hear of them. And yet this supposed honour, popular applause, desire of immortality by this means, pride and vain-glory spurs them on many times rashly and unadvisedly to make away themselves and multitudes of others. Alexander was sorry because there were no more worlds for him to conquer, he is admired by some for it; 'twas spoken like a Prince; but aswise Seneca censures him, 'twas spoken like a bedlam fool: and that sentence which the same Seneca appropriates to his father Philip and him, I apply to them all, they did as much mischief to mortal men as fire and water, those merciless elements when they rage. Which is yet more to be lamented, they persuade them this hellish course of life is holy, they promise heaven to such as venture their lives in holy war, and that by these bloody wars, (as Persians, Greeks, and Romans of old, as modern Turks do now their Commons, to encourage them to fight, that they may die in bliss), *if they die in the field, they go directly to heaven, and shall be canonised for saints*, (O diabolical invention!).

The virtue of great men

Crime, when it is prosperous and successful, is called virtue. We measure all, as Turks do, by the event, and most part as Cyprian

* The lowest class of Roman citizen

notes, in all ages, countries, places, the foulness of the fact vindicates the offender. One is crowned for that which another is tormented, made a Knight, a Lord, an Earl, a great Duke, (as Agrippa notes), for which another should have hung in gibbets, as a terror to the rest. A poor sheep stealer is hanged for stealing of victuals, compelled peradventure by necessity of that intolerable cold, hunger, and thirst, to save himself from starving: but a great man in office may securely rob whole provinces, undo thousands, pill and poll, oppress at his pleasure, flay, grind, tyrannize, enrich himself by the spoils of the Commons, be uncontrollable in his actions, and, after all, be recompensed with turgent* titles, honoured for his good service, and no man dare to find fault, or mutter at it.

The world

What's the market? A place, according to Anacharsis, wherein they cozen one another, a trap, nay, what's the world itself? A vast Chaos, a confusion of manners, as fickle as the air, a crazy house, a turbulent troop full of impurities, a mart of walking spirits, goblins, the theatre of hypocrisy, a shop of knavery, flattery, a nursery of villainy, the scene of babbling, the school of giddiness, the academy of vice; a warfare where, willing or unwilling, one must fight and either conquer or succumb, in which kill or be killed: wherein every man is for himself, his private ends, and stands upon his own guard.

Unequal rewards

To see a scholar crouch and creep to an illiterate peasant for a meal's meat; a scrivener better paid for an obligation; a falconer receive greater wages than a student: a lawyer get more in a day than a philosopher in a year, better reward for an hour than a scholar for a twelve month's study; him that can paint Thais, play on a fiddle, curl hair, etc., sooner get preferment than a

* Turgid

philologer or a poet! [...] To see a poor fellow, or an hired servant, venture his life for his new master, that will scarce give him his wages at year's end; a country colone* toil and moil, till and drudge, for a prodigal idle drone, that devours all the gain, or lasciviously consumes with phantastical expenses; a noble man in a bravado to encounter death and for a small flash of honour to cast away himself; a worldling tremble at an executioner, and yet not fear hell-fire; to wish and hope for immortality, desire to be happy, and yet by all means avoid death, a necessary passage to bring him to it!

Holland and England compared

[I]f some travellers should see (to come nearer home) those rich United Provinces of Holland, Zealand etc., over against us; those neat cities and populous towns, full of most industrious artifices, so much land recovered from the sea, and so painfully preserved by those artificial inventions, so wonderfully approved as that of Bemster in Holland, so that you would find nothing equal to it or like it in the whole world, saith Bertius the Geographer, all the world cannot match it, so many navigable channels from place to place, made by men's hands, etc., and on the other side so many thousand acres of our fens lie drowned, our cities thin, and those vile, poor, and ugly to behold in respect of theirs, our trades decayed, our still running rivers stopped, and that beneficial use of transportation wholly neglected, so many havens void of ships and towns, so many parks and forests for pleasure, barren heaths, so many villages depopulated, etc., I think sure he would find some fault. [...] The Low Countries generally have three cities at least for one of ours, and those far more populous and rich: and what is the cause, but their industry and excellency in all manner of trades; their commerce, which is maintained by a multitude of tradesmen, so many excellent channels made by art, and opportune

* Peasant

14

havens, to which they build their cities? all which we have in like measure, or at least may have. [...] 'Tis our Indies, an epitome of China, and all by reason of their industry, good policy, and commerce. Industry is a lodestone to draw all good things; that alone makes countries flourish, cities populous, and will enforce by reason of much manure, which necessarily follows, a barren soil to be fertile and good, as sheep, saith Dion, mend a bad pasture.

Our national idleness

We send our best commodities beyond the seas, which they make good use of to their necessities, set themselves a work about, and severally improve, sending the same back to us at dear rates, or else make toys and baubles of the tails of them, which they sell to us again, at as great a reckoning as they bought the whole. In most of our cities, some few excepted, like Spanish loiterers, we live wholly by tippling; inns and ale-houses, malting, are their best ploughs; their greatest traffick to sell ale. Meteran and some others object to us, that we are no whit so industrious as the Hollanders: *Manual trades* (saith he) *which are more curious or troublesome, are wholly exercised by strangers: they dwell in a sea full of fish, but they are so idle they will not catch so much as shall serve their own turns, but buy it of their neighbours.* Tush! The sea is free, they fish under our noses, and sell it to us when they have done, at their own prices. I am ashamed to hear this objected by strangers, and know not how to answer it.

Amongst our Towns, there is only London that bears the face of a City, Epitome of Britain, a famous market-place, second to none beyond seas, a noble mart: but it only grows at the expense of other cities; and yet, in my slender judgement, defective in many things. The rest (some few excepted), are in mean estate, ruinous most part, poor and full of beggars, by reason of their decayed trades, neglected or bad policy, idleness of their inhabitants, riot, which had rather beg or loiter, and be ready to starve, than work.

Burton's Utopia

I will yet, to satisfy and please myself, make a Utopia of my own, a new Atlantis, a poetical Commonwealth of mine own, in which I will freely domineer, build cities, make laws, statutes, as I list myself. And why may I not? [...]

In every so built city, I will have convenient churches, and separate-places to bury the dead in, not in church-yards; a citadel (in some, not all) to command it, prisons for offenders, opportune market-places of all sorts, for corn, meat, cattle, fuel, fish, etc., commodious courts of justice, publick halls for all societies, bourses, meeting places, armouries, in which shall be kept engines for quenching of fire, artillery gardens, publick walks, theatres, and spacious fields allotted for all gymnicks*, sports, and honest recreations, hospitals of all kinds, for children, orphans, old folks, sick men, mad men, soldiers, pest-houses, etc., not built propitiatorily, or by gouty benefactors, who, when by fraud and rapine they have extorted all their lives, oppressed whole provinces, societies etc., give something to pious uses, build a satisfactory alms-house, school, or bridge, etc., at their last end, or before perhaps, which is no otherwise than to steal a goose, and stick down a feather, rob a thousand to relieve ten: and those hospitals so built and maintained, not by collections, benevolences, donaries†, for a set number (as in ours), just so many and no more at such a rate, but for all those who stand in need, be they more or less, and at that publick expense, and so still maintained; we are not born for ourselves alone, etc.. [...]

I will provide publick schools of all kinds, singing, dancing, fencing, etc., especially of grammar and languages, not to be taught by those tedious precepts ordinarily used, but by use, example, conversation, as travellers learn abroad, and nurses teach their children. [...]

* Athletics
† Gifts

I hate those severe, unnatural, harsh, German, French, and Venetian decrees, which exclude plebeians from honours, be they never so wise, rich, virtuous, valiant, and well qualified, they must not be patricians, but keep their own rank; this is to war against nature, – odious to God and men, I abhor it. [...]

I will suffer no beggars, rogues, vagabonds, or idle persons at all, that cannot give account of their lives how they maintain themselves. If they be impotent, lame, blind, and single, they shall be sufficiently maintained in several hospitals, built for that purpose; if married and infirm, past work, or by inevitable loss, or some such like misfortune, cast behind, by distribution of corn, house-rent free, annual pensions or money they shall be relieved, and highly rewarded for their good service they have formerly done; if able, they shall be enforced to work. *For I see no reason* (as he [Sir Thomas More] said) *why an epicure or idle drone, a rich glutton, a usurer, should live at ease and do nothing, live in honour, in all manner of pleasures, and oppress others, when as in the mean time a poor labourer, a smith, a carpenter, an husbandman, that hath spent his time in continual labour, as an ass to carry burdens, to do the commonwealth good, and without whom we cannot live, shall be left in his old age to beg or starve, and lead a miserable life worse than a jument!* *

Critics and scholars

Your supercilious criticks, grammatical triflers, notemakers, curious antiquaries, find out all the ruins of wit, gutters of folly, amongst the rubbish of old writers; and what they take they spoil, all fools with them that cannot find fault; they correct others, and are hot in a cold cause, puzzle themselves to find out how many streets in Rome, houses, gates, towers, Homer's country, Aeneas' mother, Niobe's daughters, whether Sappho was a public woman? Which came first, the egg or the hen? etc. and other things which you would try to forget if you ever knew them, as Seneca holds;

* Beast of burden

what clothes the Senators did wear in Rome, what shoes, how they sat, where they went to the close stool, how many dishes in a mess, what sauce; which for the present for an historian to relate, according to Lodovic. Vives, is very ridiculous, is to them most precious valiant stuff, they admired for it, and as proud, and triumphant, in the mean time for this discovery, as if they had won a City, or conquered a Province; as rich as if they had found a mine of gold ore. One saith, they bewray* and daub a company of books and good authors with their absurd comments, dunghill reformers, Scaliger calls them, and shew their wit in censuring others, a company of foolish notetakers, humble bees, dors[†] or beetles, they rake over all those rubbish and dunghills, and prefer a manuscript many times before the Gospel itself, the critic's treasure-house, before any treasure, and with their *Omit so and so, some read so and so, my MS. has so and so*, with their latest editions, annotations, castigations etc., make books dear, themselves ridiculous, and do nobody good; yet if a man dare oppose or contradict, they are mad, up in arms on a sudden, how many sheets are written in defence, how bitter invectives, what apologies? These are a poor vintage and mere trifles. But I dare say not more of, for, with, or against them, because I am as liable to their lash as well as others.

Burton's object

[M]y purpose and endeavour is, in the following discourse, to anatomize this humour of melancholy, through all his parts and species, as it is an habit, or an ordinary disease, and that philosophically, medicinally, to shew the causes, symptoms, and several cures of it, that it may be the better avoided. [...] If hereafter, anatomizing this surly humour, my hand slip, as an unskilful prentice I lance too deep, and cut through skin and all at unawares, make it smart, or cut awry, pardon a rude hand, an

---

* Befoul
[†] Dung beetles

unskilful knife, 'tis a most difficult thing to keep an even tone, a perpetual tenor, and not sometimes to lash out; not to write satire is the difficulty, there be so many objects to divert, inward perturbations to molest, and the very best may sometimes err; if Homer, usually so good, takes a nap, it is impossible not in so much to overshoot: it is no great sin if over a long work, sleep should steal at times.

The First Partition

Burton anatomizes the definitions, symptoms and probable causes of melancholy.

Habit or disposition?

Melancholy, the subject of our present discourse, is either in disposition or habit. In disposition, is that transitory *Melancholy* which goes and comes upon every small occasion of sorrow, need, sickness, trouble, fear, grief, passion, or perturbation of the mind, any manner of care, discontent, or thought, which causeth anguish, dullness, heaviness and vexation of spirit, any ways opposite to pleasure, mirth, joy, delight, causing forwardness, or a dislike. In which equivocal and improper sense, we call him melancholy, that is dull, sad, sour, lumpish, ill disposed, solitary, any way moved, or displeased. And from these melancholy dispositions no man living is free, no Stoic, none so wise, none so happy, none so patient, so generous, so godly, so divine, that can vindicate himself; so well-composed, but more or less, some time or other he feels the smart of it. Melancholy in this sense is the character of Mortality.

The four humours

Blood is a hot, sweet, temperate, red humour, prepared in the *meseraick** veins, and made of the most temperate parts of the *chylus* in the liver, whose office is to nourish the whole body, to give it strength and colour, being disbursed by the veins through every part of it. And from it *spirits* are first begotten in the heart, which afterwards by the *arteries* are communicated to the other parts.

Pituita, or phlegm, is a cold and moist humour, begotten of the colder parts of the *chylus* (or white juice coming out of the

* Mesenteric

meat digested in the stomack) in the liver; his office is to nourish and moisten the members of the body, which, as the tongue, are moved, that they be not over dry.

Choler is hot and dry, bitter, begotten of the hotter parts of the *chylus*, and gathered to the gall: it helps the natural heat and senses, and serves to the expelling of excrements.

Melancholy, cold and dry, thick, black, and sour, begotten of the more faeculent part of nourishment, and purged from the spleen, is a bridle to the other two hot humours, *blood* and *choler*, preserving them in the blood and nourishing the bones. These four humours have some analogy with the four elements, and to the four ages in man.

Those pre-disposed to melancholy

Such [people] as have the *Moon*, *Saturn*, *Mercury*, misaffected in their genitures; such as live in over-cold or over-hot climes: such as are born of *melancholy* parents: such as offend in those six non-natural things, are black, or of an high sanguine complexion, that have little heads, that have a hot heart, moist brain, hot liver and cold stomack, have been long sick: such as are solitary by nature, great students, given to much contemplation, lead a life out of action, are most subject to *melancholy*. Of sexes both, but men more often, yet women misaffected are far more violent and grievously troubled. Of seasons of the year, the *Autumn* is most melancholy. Of peculiar times; old age, from which natural melancholy is almost an inseparable accident; but this artificial malady is more frequent in such as are of a middle age.

Fairies

Some put our Fairies into this rank*, which have been in former times adored with much superstition, with sweeping their houses, and setting of a pail of clean water, good victuals, and the like, and then they should not be pinched, but find money in their

* Terrestrial devils

shoes, and be fortunate in their enterprises. These are they that dance on heaths and greens, as Lavater thinks with Trithemius, and, as Olaus Magnus adds, leave that green circle, which we commonly find in plain fields, which others hold to proceed from a meteor falling, or some accidental rankness of the ground; so Nature sports herself. They are sometimes seen by old women and children. Hieronymus Pauli, in his description of the city of Bercino in Spain, relates how they have been familiarly seen near that town, about fountains and hills. At times they lead simple men into their mountain retreats, where they exhibit marvellous sights, saith Trithemius, and astonish their ears by the sound of bells etc.. Giraldus Cambrensis gives instance in a Monk of Wales that was so deluded. Paracelsus reckons up many places in Germany, where they do usually walk in little coats some two foot long. A bigger kind there is of them, called with us *Hobgoblins*, and *Robin Goodfellows*, that would in those superstitious times grind corn for a mess of milk, cut wood, or do any manner of drudgery work.

The Devil

Thus the Devil reigns, and in a thousand several shapes, as a roaring lion still seeks whom he may devour, by earth, sea, land, air, as yet unconfined, though some will have his proper place the air, all that space betwixt us and the Moon for them that transgressed least, and Hell for the wickedest of them; here, as though in prison to the end of the world, afterwards thrust into the place of doom, as Austin* holds in The City of God. But be [he] where he will, he rageth while he may to comfort himself, as Lactantius thinks, with other men's falls, he labours all he can to bring them into the same pit of perdition with him. For *men's miseries, calamities, and ruins are the Devil's banqueting dishes.* By many temptations, and several engines, he seeks to captivate our souls. The Lord of lies, saith Austin, *as he was deceived himself, he seeks to*

* St Augustine

deceive others, the ring-leader to all naughtiness, as he did by Eve and Cain, Sodom and Gomorrah, so would he do by all the world. Sometimes he tempts by covetousness, drunkenness, pleasure, pride, etc., errs, dejects, saves, kills, protects, and rides some men, as they do their horses. He studies our overthrow, and generally seeks our destruction. [...] [O]f all other, melancholy persons are most subject to diabolical temptations and illusions, and most apt to entertain them, and the Devil best able to work upon them; but whether by obsession, or possession, or otherwise, I will not determine; 'tis a difficult question. Delrio the Jesuit, Springer and his colleague, Thyreus the Jesuit, Hieronymus Mengus, and others of that rank of pontifical writers, it seems, by their exorcisms and conjurations approve of it, having forged many stories to that purpose. A nun did eat a lettuce *without grace, or without signing with the sign of the cross*, and was instantly possessed. Durand relates that he saw a wench possessed in Bononia with two devils, by eating an unhallowed pomegranate, as she did afterwards confess, when she was cured by exorcisms. And therefore our papists do sign themselves so often with the sign of the cross, that the demon dare not enter, and exorcise all manner of meats, as being unclean or accursed otherwise, as Bellarmine defends. Many such stories I find amongst pontifical writers, to prove their assertions; let them free their own credits; some few I will recite in this kind out of most approved Physicians. Cornelius Gemma relates of a young maid, called Katherine Gaulter, a cooper's daughter, in the year 1571, that had such strange passions and convulsions, three men could not sometimes hold her; she purged a live eel, which he saw, a foot and a half long, and touched himself, but the eel afterwards vanished; she vomited some 24 pounds of fulsome stuff of all colours twice a day for 14 days; and after that she voided great balls of hair, pieces of wood, pigeons' dung, parchment, goose dung, coals; and after them two pounds of pure blood, and then again coals and stones, of which some had inscriptions, bigger than a walnut, some of them pieces of glass, brass, etc., besides paroxysms of laughing, weeping and ecstasies, etc.. And this (he says), I saw with horror.

Old age

After 70 years (as the Psalmist saith) *all is trouble and sorrow*; and common experience confirms the truth of it in weak and old persons, especially in such as have lived in action all their lives, had great employment, much business, much command, and many servants to oversee, and leave off as Charles the Fifth did to King Philip, resign up all on a sudden. They are overcome with melancholy in an instant: or, if they do continue in such courses, they dote at last, (an old man is twice a boy), and are not able to manage their estates through common infirmities incident in their age; full of ache, sorrow, and grief, children again, dizzards*, they carl† many times as they sit, and talk to themselves, they are angry, waspish, displeased with every thing, *suspicious of all, wayward, covetous, hard,* (saith Tully) *self-willed, superstitious, self-conceited, braggers, and admirers of themselves.*

Parental inheritance

Foolish, drunken, or hare-brain women most part bring forth children like unto themselves, morose and languid, and so likewise he that lies with a menstruous woman. Excessive venery, which Lemnius especially condemneth in sailors, who enter in unto their wives without regard to this, and without observing the interlunary period, is a principal cause of great injury [...] and, moreover, those luckless ones begotten at this period of lunar influence are commonly mad, doting, stupid, ailing, filthy, impotent, plague-ridden, of the lowest vitality, and robbed of all strength of mind and body; born to labour, though lords themselves, saith Eustathius, as were Hercules and others.

* Idiots
† Act churlishly

The Jews bitterly inveigh against this foul and filthy coupling amongst Christians; they abhor it as unlawful, and prohibit it amongst their own people. And because Christians so often are leprous, raving, debilitated, scabby, since there are so many diseases, white spots, itch, skin and facial blotches, so many contagious pestilences, painful and malignant, they charge it to this impure intercourse, and call those men bloody in their pledges, who, when the impurity of the month is discharging, do not abhor coupling. 'Twas once condemned by Divine Law, men of this habit punished by death; the father stoned, if children were deformed, for that he kept not himself from an unclean woman.

Dietary prohibitions

Beef, a strong and hearty meat (cold in the first degree, dry in the second, saith Galen) is condemned by him, and all succeeding authors, to breed gross melancholy blood: good for such as are sound, and of a strong constitution, for labouring men, if ordered aright, corned, young, of an ox (for all gelded meats in every species are held best) or if old, such as have been tired out with labour, are preferred. Aubanus and Sabellicus commend Portugal beef to be the most savoury, best and easiest of digestion; we commend ours: but all is rejected and unfit for such as lead a resty life, any ways inclined to Melancholy, or dry of complexion.[…]

Milk, and all that comes of milk, as butter and cheese, curds, etc. increase melancholy (whey only excepted, which is most wholesome): some except asses' milk. The rest, to such as are sound, is nutritive and good, especially for young children, but because soon turned to corruption, not good for those that have unclean stomacks, are subject to headache, or have green wounds, stone, etc.. Of all cheeses, I take that kind which we call Banbury cheese to be the best. The older, stronger, and harder, the worst, as Langius discourseth in his Epistle to Melancthon, cited by Mizaldus, Isaac, Galen etc..

Amongst fowl, peacocks and pigeons, all fenny fowl are forbidden, as ducks, geese, swans, herns, cranes, coots, dipadders*, waterhens, with all those teals, curs, sheldrakes, and peckled[†] fowls, that come hither in winter out of Scandia, Muscovy, Greenland, Friezland, which half the year are covered over with snow, and frozen up. Though these be fair in feathers, pleasant in taste, and have a good out-side, like hypocrites, white in plumes, and soft, their flesh is hard, black, unwholesome, dangerous, melancholy meat; they load and putrefy the stomack, saith Isaac. Their young ones are more tolerable, but young pigeons he quite disapproves. [...]

Amongst herbs to be eaten, I find gourds, cowcumbers, coleworts[‡], melons, disallowed, but especially cabbage. It causeth troublesome dreams, and sends up black vapours to the brain. Galen of all herbs condemns cabbage; and Isaac, it brings heaviness to the soul. Some are of opinion that all raw herbs and sallets breed melancholy blood, except bugloss and lettuce. Crato speaks against all herbs and worts, except borage, bugloss, fennel, parsley, dill, balm, succory[§]. Magninus all herbs are simply evil to feed on (as he thinks). So did that scoffing cook in Plautus hold,

Like other cooks I do not supper dress,
    That put whole meadows into a platter,
And make no better of their guests than beeves,
    With herbs and grass to feed them fatter.

Drink a cause of melancholy

All black wines, overhot, compound, strong thick drinks, as Muscadine, Malmsey, Alicant, Rumney, Brown Bastard,

---

* Dabchicks
[†] Speckled
[‡] Kales
[§] Chicory

Metheglin, and the like, of which they have thirty several kinds in Muscovy, all such made drinks are hurtful in this case, to such as are hot, or of a sanguine cholerick complexion, young, or inclined to head-melancholy. For many times the drinking of wine alone causeth it. Arculanus puts in wine for a great cause, especially if immoderately used. Guianerius tells a story of two Dutchmen, to whom he gave entertainment in his house, *that in one month's space were both melancholy by drinking of wine*, one did nought but sing, the other sigh.[…] Yet notwithstanding all this, to such as are cold, or sluggish melancholy, a cup of wine is good physick, and so doth Mercurialis grant. […] Beer, if it be over new or over stale, over strong, or not sod, smell of the cask, sharp, or sour, is most unwholesome, frets and galls, etc.. Henricus Ayrerus, in a consultation of his, for one that laboured of *hypochondriacal* melancholy, discommends beer. So doth Crato, in that excellent counsel of his, as too windy, because of the hop. But he means belike that thick black Bohemian beer brewed in some parts of Germany.

Nothing comes in so thick
Nothing goes out so thin,
It must needs follow then
The dregs are left within.

As that old Poet scoffed, calling it a monstrous drink, like the River Styx. But let them say as they list, to such as are accustomed unto it, *'tis a most wholesome* (so Polydore Virgil calleth it) *and a pleasant drink*, it is more subtle and better for the hop that rarefies it, hath an especial virtue against melancholy, as our Herbalists confess, Fuchsius approves, and many others.

Quantity of food

There is not so much harm proceeding from the substance itself of the meat, and quality of it, in ill dressing and preparing, as there is from the quantity, disorder of time and place, unseasonable use of it, intemperance, overmuch or over little taking of it. A true saying it is, this gluttony kills more than the sword, this all-devouring and murdering gut. And that of Pliny is truer, *simple diet is the best; heaping up of several meats is pernicious, and sauces worse; many dishes bring many diseases.* Avicenna cries out that *nothing is worse than to feed on many dishes, or protract the time of meals longer than ordinary; from thence proceed our infirmities, and 'tis the fountain of all diseases, which arise out of the repugnancy of gross humours.* Thence, saith Fernelius, come crudities, wind, oppilations*, *cacochymia, plethora, cachexia, bradypepsia,* sudden death, intestate old age, and what not.

As a lamp is choked with a multitude of oil, or a little fire with overmuch wood quite extinguished; so is the natural heat with immoderate eating strangled in the body. An insatiable paunch, one saith, is a pernicious sink, and the fountain of all diseases, both of body and mind.[...] And yet for all this harm, which apparently follows surfeiting and drunkenness, see how we luxuriate and rage in this kind. Read what Johannes Stuckius hath written lately of this subject, in his great volumes *The Feasts of Olden Times,* and of our present age; what prodigious suppers; those who invite us to supper but bring us to our tomb! What *Fagos, Epicures, Apicii, Heliogabali,* our times afford! Lucullus' ghost walks still, and every man desires to sup in *Apollo*[†]. Æsop's costly dish is ordinarily served up. Those things please most which cost most. The dearest cates[‡] are best, and 'tis an ordinary thing to bestow twenty or thirty pound on a dish, some thousand crown upon a dinner. Muley-Hamet, King of Fez and Morocco, spent three pounds on the sauce of a capon: it is nothing in our times, we scorn all that is cheap. *We loathe the very light* (some of us, as Seneca notes) *because it comes free, and we are offended with the sun's heat, and those cool blasts, because we buy them not.* This air

* Obstructions

† A rich chamber in Lucullus' house

‡ Dishes

we breathe is so common, *we care not for it*; nothing pleaseth but what is dear. And if we be witty in anything, it is for the gullet's sake: if we study at all, it is the study of debauchery, to please the palate, and to satisfy the gut. *A cook of old was a base knave* (as Livy complains) *but now a great man in request: cookery is become an art, a noble science: cooks are Gentlemen:* Belly is God. They wear *their brains in their bellies, and their guts in their heads;* as Agrippa taxed some rich parasites of his time, rushing on their own destruction, as if a man should run upon the point of a sword, they eat till they burst: all day, all night, let the Physician say what he will, imminent danger and feral* diseases are now ready to seize upon them, they will eat till they vomit, and vomit to eat again, saith Seneca;[…] or till they burst again. They load their bellies with the carnage of animals, and rake over all the world, as so many slaves, belly-gods, and land-serpents; the whole world cannot satisfy their appetites. *Sea, Land, Rivers, Lakes, etc., may not give content to their raging guts.* To make up the mess, what immoderate drinking in every place! A drunken old woman drags a drunken old man, how they flock to the Tavern! as if they were born to no other end but to eat and drink, like Offellius Bibulus, that famous Roman Parasite, who while he lived was either taking in wine or pissing it off. […] And what vices are now considered virtues: 'tis now the fashion of our times, an honour: 'tis now come to that pass, (as Chrysostom comments) that he is no Gentleman, a very milk-sop, a clown, of no bringing-up, that will not drink, fit for no company; he is your only gallant that plays it off finest, no disparagement now to stagger in the streets, reel, rave, etc., but much to his fame and renown. *Our Dutchmen invite all comers with a pail and a dish.* They drain inexhaustible noggins even as a funnel, and from monstrous vessels they pour them into their more monstrous selves, *making barrels of their bellies.* 'Tis incredible to say, as one of their own country-men complains, how much liquor that most immoderate race will take, etc.. *How*

* Fatal

they love a man that will be drunk, crown him and honour him for it, hate him that will not pledge him, stab him, kill him: a most intolerable offense and not to be forgiven!

Venery – too little and too much

Matthiolus *avoucheth of his knowledge, that some through bashfulness abstained from Venery, and thereupon became very heavy and dull; and some others, that were very timorous, melancholy, and beyond all measure sad.* Oribasius speaks of some, *that, if they do not use carnal copulation, are continually troubled with heaviness and headache; and some in the same case by intermission of it.*[...] Villanovanus saith he *knew many monks and widows grievously troubled with melancholy, and that from this sole cause.* Lodovicus Mercatus, and Rodericus à Castro treat largely of this subject, and will have it produce a peculiar kind of melancholy in stale maids, nuns, and widows; on account of suppressed menses, and omission of venery, they are timid, unhappy, anxious, sheepish, mistrustful, listless, without purpose at the very height of life, and despairing of more favourable circumstances, they are melancholy in the highest degree and all for want of husbands.[...]

Intemperate *Venus* is all out as bad in the other extreme. Galen reckons up melancholy amongst those diseases which are *exasperated by venery:* so doth Avicenna, Oribasius, Marsilius Cognatus, Montaltus, Guianerius. Magninus gives the reason because *it infrigidates and dries up the body, consumes the spirits;* and would therefore have all such as are cold and dry to take heed of and to avoid it as a mortal enemy. Jacchinus ascribes the same cause, and instanceth a Patient of his, that married a young wife in a hot summer, *and so dried himself with chamber-work, that he became in short space, from melancholy, mad:* he cured him by moistening remedies.

Idleness

Nothing so good, but it may be abused. Nothing better than exercise (if opportunely used) for the preservation of the body:

nothing so bad, if it be unseasonable, violent, or overmuch. […] Opposite to exercise is idleness (the badge of gentry) or want of exercise, the bane of body and mind, the nurse of naughtiness, stepmother of discipline, the chief author of all mischief, one of the seven deadly sins, and a sole cause of this and many other maladies, the devil's cushion, as Gualter calls it, his pillow and chief reposal. *For the mind can never rest, but still meditates on one thing or other; except it be occupied about some honest business, of his own accord it rusheth into melancholy. As too much and violent exercise offends on the one side, so doth an idle life on the other,* (saith Crato) *it fills the body full of phlegm, gross humours, and all manner of obstructions, rheums, catarrhs etc.* […]

As fern grows in untilled grounds, and all manner of weeds, so do gross humours in an idle body. A horse in a stable that never travels, a hawk in a mew that seldom flies, are both subject to diseases; which, left unto themselves, are most free from any such incumbrances. An idle dog will be mangy, and how shall an idle person think to escape? Idleness of the mind is much worse than this of the body; wit without employment is a disease, the rust of the soul, a plague, a hell itself, the greatest danger to the soul, Galen calls it. *As in a standing pool worms and filthy creepers increase,* (the water itself putrefies, and air likewise, if it be not continually stirred by the wind), *so do evil and corrupt thoughts in an idle person,* the soul is contaminated. In a Commonwealth, where is no publick enemy, there is, likely, civil wars, and they rage upon themselves: this body of ours, when it is idle, and knows not how to bestow itself, macerates and vexeth itself with cares, griefs, false fears, discontents, and suspicions; it tortures and preys upon its own bowels, and is never at rest. Thus much I dare boldly say, he or she that is idle, be they of what condition they will, never so rich, so well allied, fortunate, happy, let them have all things in abundance, and felicity, that heart can wish and desire, all contentment; so long as he or she or they are idle, they shall never be pleased, never well in body and mind, but weary, sickly still, vexed still, loathing still, weeping, sighing, grieving, suspecting, offended with the world, with every object, wishing themselves gone or dead, or else carried away with some foolish phantasy or other. And this is the true cause that so many great men, Ladies, and Gentlewomen, labour of this disease in Country and City; for idleness is an appendix to nobility, they count it a disgrace to work, and spend all their days in sports, recreations, and pastimes, and will therefore take no pains, be of no vocation: they feed liberally, fare well, want exercise, action, employment, (for to work, I say, they may not abide), and company to their desires, and thence their bodies become full of gross humours, wind, crudities, their minds disquieted, dull, heavy, etc.. Care, jealousy, fear of some diseases, sullen fits, weeping fits, seize too familiarly on them. For what will not fear and phantasy work in an idle body? what distempers will they not cause? When the children of Israel murmured against Pharaoh in Egypt, he commanded his officers to double their task, and let them get straw themselves, and yet make their full number of bricks; for the sole cause why they mutiny, and are evil at ease, is, *they are idle*. When you shall hear and see so many discontented persons in all places where you come, so many several grievances, unnecessary complaints, fear, suspicions, the best means to redress it is to set them awork, so to busy their minds; for the truth is, they are idle. Well they may build castles in the air for a time, and soothe up themselves with phantastical and pleasant humours, but in the end they will prove as bitter as gall, they shall be still I say discontent, suspicious, fearful, jealous, sad, fretting and vexing of themselves; so long as they be idle, it is impossible to please them. As that A. Gellius could observe: he that knows not how to spend his time, hath more business, care, grief, anguish of mind, than he that is most busy in the midst of all his business. An idle person (as he follows it) knows not when he is well, what he would have, or whither he would go. He is tired out with everything, displeased with all, weary of his life: neither well at home nor abroad, he wanders, and lives, beside himself. In a word, what the mischievous effects of laziness and idleness are, I do not find anywhere more accurately expressed, than in these verses of Philolaches in the Comical Poet, which for their elegancy, I will part insert [and paraphrase]: – *A young man is like a fair new house, the carpenter leaves it well built, in good repair, of solid stuff; but a bad tenant lets rain in, and for want of reparation fall to decay, etc..* Our Parents, Tutors, Friends, spare no cost to bring us up in our youth in all manner of virtuous education; but when we are left to ourselves, idleness as a tempest drives all virtuous notions out of our minds, and, on a sudden, by sloth and such bad ways, we come to naught.

Solitariness

Cousin-german to idleness, and a concomitant cause, which goes hand in hand with it, is too much solitariness, by the testimony of all Physicians, cause and symptom both; but as it is here put for a cause, it is either coact, enforced, or else voluntary. Enforced solitariness is commonly seen in Students, Monks, Friars, Anchorites, that by their order and course of life must abandon all company, society of other men and betake themselves to a private cell: the seclusion of excessive idleness as Bale and Hospinian well term it, such as are the Carthusians of our time, that eat no flesh (by their order), keep perpetual silence, never go abroad; such as live in prison, or some desert place, and cannot have company, as many of our Country Gentlemen do in solitary houses, they must either be alone without companions, or live beyond their means, and entertain all comers as so many hosts, or else converse with their servants and hinds*, such as are unequal, inferior to them, and of a contrary disposition; or else, as some do to avoid solitariness, spend their time with lewd fellows in taverns, and in ale-houses, and thence addict themselves to some unlawful disports, or dissolute courses. Divers again are cast upon this rock of solitariness for want of means,

* Farm workers

or out of a strong apprehension of some infirmity, disgrace, or through bashfulness, rudeness, simplicity, they cannot apply themselves to others' company. To the unhappy man nothing is dearer than solitude, where there is none to reproach him for his misery. This enforced solitariness takes place, and produceth his effect soonest, in such as have spent their time jovially, peradventure in all honest recreations, in good company, in some great family or populous City, and are upon a sudden confined to a desert Country Cottage far off, restrained of their liberty, and barred from their ordinary associates: solitariness is very irksome to such, most tedious, and a sudden sense of great inconvenience.

Voluntary solitariness is that which is familiar with Melancholy, and gently brings on like a Siren, a shoeing-horn, or some Sphinx, to this irrevocable gulf, a primary cause Piso calls it; most pleasant it is at first, to such as are melancholy given, to lie in bed whole days, and keep their chambers, to walk alone in some solitary Grove, betwixt Wood and Water, by a Brook side, to meditate upon some delightsome and pleasant subject, which shall affect them most; happy madness and delightful illusion. A most incomparable delight it is to melancholize, and build castles in the air, to go smiling to themselves, acting an infinite variety of parts, which they suppose and strongly imagine they represent, or that they see acted or done.[...] So pleasant their vain conceits are, that they hinder their ordinary tasks and necessary business, they cannot address themselves to them, or almost to any study or employment, these phantastical and bewitching thoughts so covertly, so feelingly, so urgently, so continually, set upon, creep in, insinuate, possess, overcome, distract, and detain them, they cannot, I say, go about their more necessary business, stave off or extricate themselves, but are ever musing, melancholizing, and carried along, as (they say) that is led round about an heath with a *Puck* in the night, they run earnestly on in this labyrinth of anxious and solicitous melancholy meditations, and cannot well or willingly refrain, or easily leave off, winding and unwinding themselves, as so many clocks, and still pleasing their humours, until at last the scene is turned upon a sudden, by some bad object, and they, being now habituated to such vain meditations and solitary places, can endure no company, can ruminate of nothing but harsh and distasteful subjects. Fear, sorrow, suspicion, clownish timidity, discontent, cares, and weariness of life surprise them in a moment, and they can think of nothing else; continually suspecting, no sooner are their eyes open, but this infernal plague of Melancholy seizeth on them, and terrifies their souls, representing some dismal object to their minds, which now by no means, no labour, no persuasions, they can avoid, the deadly arrow yet remains in their side, they may not be rid of it, they cannot resist.

Abbeys and Monasteries

I may not deny but that there is some profitable meditation, contemplation, and kind of solitariness to be embraced, which the Fathers so highly commended, Hierom, Chrysostom, Cyprian, Austin, in whole tracts, which Petrarch, Erasmus, Stella, and others, so much magnify in their books; a Paradise, a Heaven on earth, if it be used aright, good for the body, and better for the soul: as many of those old Monks used it, to divine contemplations. [...] Methinks, therefore, our too zealous innovators were not so well advised, in that general subversion of Abbies and Religious Houses, promiscuously to fling down all. They might have taken away those gross abuses crept in amongst them, rectified such inconveniences, and not so far to have raved and raged against those fair buildings, and everlasting monuments of our forefather's devotion, consecrated to pious uses. Some Monasteries and Collegiate Cells might have been well spared, and their revenues otherwise employed, here and there one, in good Towns or Cities at least, for men and women of all sorts and conditions to live in, to sequester themselves from the cares and tumults of the world, that were not desirous or fit to marry, or otherwise willing to be troubled with common affairs, and knew not well where to bestow themselves, to live apart in, for more conveniency, good education, better company sake, to follow their studies (I say) to the perfection of arts and sciences, common good, and, as some truly devoted Monks of old had done, freely and truly to serve God.

Imagination

Avicenna speaks of one that could cast himself into a palsy when he list; and some can imitate the tunes of birds and beasts, that they can hardly be discerned. Dagobertus' and Saint Francis' scars and wounds, like to those of Christ's (if at the least any such were), Agrippa supposeth to have happened by force of imagination. That some are turned to wolves, from men to women, and women again to men (which is constantly believed) to the same imagination: or from men to asses, dogs, or any other shapes; Wierus ascribes all those famous transformations to imagination. That in *Hydrophobia* they seem to see the picture of a dog still in their water, that melancholy men and sick men, conceive so many phantastical visions, apparitions to themselves, and have such absurd suppositions, as that they are Kings, Lords, cocks, bears, apes, owls; that they are heavy, light, transparent, great and little, senseless and dead […] can be imputed to naught else but to a corrupt, false, and violent imagination. It works not in sick and melancholy men only, but even most forcibly sometimes in such as are sound: it makes them suddenly sick, and alters their temperature, in an instant. And sometimes a strong conceit or apprehension, as Valesius proves, will take away diseases: in both kinds it will produce real effects. Men, if they see but another man tremble, giddy, or sick of some fearful disease. Or if by some soothsayer, wiseman, fortune-teller, or physician, they be told they have such a disease, they will so seriously apprehend it, that they will instantly labour of it. A thing familiar in China (saith Riccius the Jesuit): *if it be told them they shall be sick on such a day, when that day comes, they will surely be sick, and will be so terribly afflicted, that sometimes they die upon it.*[...] So diversely doth this phantasy of ours affect, turn and wind, so imperiously command our bodies, which, as another *Proteus, or a Chameleon, can take all shapes; and is of such force* (as Ficinus adds) *that it can work upon others as well as ourselves.* How can otherwise blear eyes in one man cause the like affection in another? Why doth one man's yawning make another yawn; one man's pissing provoke a second many times to do the like? Why doth scraping of trenchers offend a third, or hacking of files? Why doth a carkass bleed, when the murderer is brought before it, some weeks after the murder hath been done?

Fear

Many lamentable effects this fear causeth in men, as to be red, pale, tremble, sweat, it makes sudden cold and heat to come over all the body, palpitation of the heart, syncope etc.. It amazeth many men that are to speak, or shew themselves in publick assemblies, or before some great personages, as Tully confessed of himself, that he trembled still at the beginning of his speech; and Demosthenes that great Orator of Greece before Philip. It confounds voice and memory, as Lucian wittily brings in Jupiter Tragœdus so much afraid of his auditory, when he was to make a speech to the rest of the Gods, that he could not utter a ready word, but was compelled to use Mercury's help in prompting. Many men are so amazed and astonished with fear, they know not where they are, what they say, what they do, and that which is worst, it tortures them many days before with continual affrights and suspicion. It hinders most honourable attempts, and makes their hearts ache, sad and heavy. They that live in fear are never free, resolute, secure, never merry, but in continual pain: that, as Vives truly said, no greater misery, no rack, no torture like unto it; ever suspicious, anxious, solicitous, they are childishly drooping without reason, without judgement, *especially if some terrible object be offered*, as Plutarch hath it.

Disgrace

Shame and disgrace cause most violent passions, and bitter pangs. Generous minds are often moved with shame to despair for some publick disgrace. And *he*, saith Philo, *that subjects himself to fear, grief, ambition, shame, is not happy, but altogether miserable, tortured with continual labour, care, and misery.* It is as forcible a batterer as any of the rest. *Many men neglect the tumults of the world, and care not for glory, and yet they are afraid of infamy, repulse, disgrace; they can severely contemn pleasure, bear grief indifferently, but they are quite battered and broken with reproach and obloquy*; and so are dejected many times for some publick injury, disgrace, as a box on the ear by their inferior, to be overcome by their adversary, foiled in the field, to be out in a speech, some foul fact committed or disclosed, etc., that they dare not come abroad all their lives after, but melancholize in corners, and keep in holes. The most generous spirits are most subject to it. [...] A grave and learned Minister, and an ordinary Preacher at Alkmaar in Holland, was (one day as he walked in the fields for his recreation) suddenly taken with a lask* or looseness, and thereupon compelled to retire to the next ditch; but being surprised at unawares by some Gentlewomen of his Parish wandering that way, was so abashed, that he did never after shew his head in publick, or come into the Pulpit, but pined away with Melancholy. So shame amongst other passions can play his prize.

Envy

As a moth gnaws a garment, so, saith Chrysostom, *doth envy consume a man.* [...] He tortures himself if his equal, friend, neighbour, be preferred, commended, do well, if he understand of it, it galls him afresh, and no greater pain can come to him than to hear of another man's well-doing, 'tis a dagger at his heart every such object. He looks at him, as they that fell down in Lucian's rock of honour, with an envious eye, and will damage himself to

* Diarrhoea

39

do another mischief. As he did in Æsop, lose one eye willingly, that his fellow might lose both, or that rich man in Quintilian, that poisoned the flowers in his garden, because his neighbour's bees should get no more honey from them. His whole life is sorrow, and every word he speaks a *satire*, nothing fats him but other men's ruins. For, to speak in a word, envy is naught else but sorrow for other men's good, be it present, past, or to come: and joy at their harms, opposite to mercy, which grieves at other men's mischances, and mis-affects the body in another kind; so Damascen defines it and we find it true. 'Tis a common disease and almost natural to us, as Tacitus holds, to envy another man's prosperity. And 'tis in most men an incurable disease.

Emulation

Every society, corporation, and private family, is full of it, it takes hold almost of all sorts of men, from the Prince to the Ploughman, even amongst Gossips it is to be seen; scarce three in a company but there is siding, faction, emulation, between two of them, some dissension, jar, private grudge, heart-burning, in the midst of them. Scarce two Gentlemen dwell together in the Country, (if they be not near kin or linked in marriage), but there is emulation betwixt them and their servants, some quarrel or some grudge betwixt their wives or children, friends or followers, some contention about wealth, gentry, precedency, etc. by means of which, like the frog in Æsop, *that would swell till she was as big as an ox, burst her self at last*, they will stretch beyond their fortunes, callings and strive so long, that they consume their substance in lawsuits, or otherwise in hospitality, feasting, fine clothes, to get a few bombast titles, for we all vie with one another in our ostentatious poverty; to out-brave one another, they will tire their bodies, macerate their souls, and through contentions or mutual invitations beggar themselves. Scarce two great Scholars in an age, but with bitter invectives they fall foul one on the other, and their adherents; Scotists, Thomists, Realists, Nominalists,

Platonists, and Aristotelians, Galenists and Paracelsians, etc.. It holds in all professions.

Honest emulation in studies, in all callings, is not to be disliked, 'tis, as one calls it, the whetsone of wit, the nurse of wit and valour, and those noble Romans out of this spirit did brave exploits. There is a modest ambition, as Themistocles was roused up with the glory of Miltiades, Achilles' trophies moved Alexander.

> *'Tis silly impudence to strive ever;*
> *But idle conceit to strive never.*
> – *Grotius*

'Tis a sluggish humour not to emulate or to sue at all, to withdraw himself, neglect, refrain from such places, honours, offices, through sloth, niggardliness, fear, bashfulness, or otherwise to which by his birth, place, fortunes, education, he is called, apt, fit, and well able to undergo; but when it is immoderate, it is a plague and a miserable pain. What a deal of money did Henry the 8, and Francis the First, King of France, spend at that famous interview! and how many vain Courtiers, seeking each to outbrave other, spent themselves, their livelihood and fortunes, and died beggars! Adrian the Emperor was so galled with it, that he killed all his equals; so did Nero. [...]

This hatred, malice, faction, and desire of revenge, invented first all those racks, and wheels, strappadoes, brazen bulls, feral engines, prisons, inquisitions, severe laws, to macerate and torment one another. How happy might we be, and end our time with blessed days and sweet content, if we could contain ourselves, and, as we ought to do, put up injuries, learn humility, meekness, patience, forget and forgive, as in God's word we are enjoined, compose such small controversies amongst ourselves, moderate our passions in this kind, *and think better of others*, as Paul would have us, *than of ourselves: be of like affection one towards another, and not avenge ourselves, but have peace with all men!* But being that we are so peevish and perverse, insolent and proud, so factious and seditious, so malicious and envious, we do by turns harass, maul and vex one another, torture, disquiet, and precipitate ourselves into that gulf of woes and cares, aggravate our misery and melancholy, heap upon us hell and eternal damnation.

Discontents

One is miserable, another ridiculous, a third odious. One complains of this grievance, another of that: now the head aches, then the feet, now the lungs, then the liver, etc.; he is rich, but base born; he is noble, but poor; a third hath means, but he wants health, peradventure, or wit to manage his estate. Children vex one, wife a second, etc.. No man is pleased with his fortune, a pound of sorrow is familiarly mixt with a dram of content, little or no joy, little comfort, but everywhere danger, contention, anxiety in all places. Go where thou wilt, and thou shalt find discontents, cares, woes, complaints, sickness, diseases, incumbrances, exclamations. […]

Who can endure the miseries of it? *In prosperity we are insolent and intolerable, dejected in adversity, in all fortunes foolish and miserable. In adversity I wish for prosperity, and in prosperity I am afraid of adversity. What mediocrity may be found? where is no temptation? what condition of life is free? Wisdom hath labour annexed to it, glory envy; riches and cares, children and incumbrances, pleasure and diseases, rest and beggary, go together: as if a man were therefore born,* (as the Platonists hold), *to be punished in this life for some precedent sins;* or that, as Pliny complains, *Nature may be rather accounted a stepmother than a mother unto us, all things considered. No creature's life so brittle, so full of fear, so mad, so furious; only man is plagued with envy, discontent, griefs, covetousness, ambition, superstition.* Our whole life is an Irish Sea, wherein there is naught to be expected but tempestuous storms and troublesome waves, and those infinite;

So great a sea of troubles do I see,
That to swim out from it does seem impossible;
   – Euripides

no Halcyonian times, wherein a man can hold himself secure, or agree with his present estate: but, as Boethius infers, *there is something in every one of us, which before trial we seek, and having tried abhor: we earnestly wish, and eagerly covet, and are eftsoons weary of it.* Thus betwixt hope and fear, suspicions, angers, betwixt falling in, falling out, etc., we bangle away our best days, befool out our times, we lead a contentious, discontent, tumultuous, melancholy, miserable life; insomuch, that if we could foretell what was to come, and put it to our choice, we should rather refuse than accept of this painful life. In a word, the world itself is a maze, a labyrinth of errors, a desert, a wilderness, a den of thieves, cheaters, etc., full of filthy puddles, horrid rocks, precipices, an ocean of adversity, an heavy yoke, wherein infirmities and calamities overtake and follow one another, as the sea waves; and if we scape Scylla, we fall foul on Charybdis, and so, in perpetual fear, labour, anguish, we run from one plague, one mischief, one burden, to another, serving a hard servitude, and you may as soon separate weight from lead, heat from fire, moistness from water, brightness from the sun, as misery, discontent, care, calamity, danger, from a man.

Self-love

Self-love, Pride and Vain-glory, which Chrysostom calls one of the devil's three great nets; Bernard, *an arrow which pierceth the soul through, and slays it; a sly insensible enemy, not perceived,* are main causes. Where neither anger, lust, covetousness, fear, sorrow, etc. nor any other perturbation can lay hold, this will slily and insensibly pervert us. Those, (saith Cyprian) whom surfeiting could not overtake, self-love hath overcome. *He that hath scorned all money, bribes, gifts, upright otherwise and sincere, hath inserted himself to no fond imagination, and sustained all those tyrannical concupiscences of the body, hath lost all his honour, captivated by vain-glory.* It consumes both mind and heart. A great assault and cause of our present malady, although we do most part neglect, take no notice of it, yet this is a violent batterer of our souls, causeth melancholy and dotage. This pleasing humour, this soft and whispering popular air, this delectable frenzy, most irrefragable passion, this delightful illusion, this acceptable disease, which so sweetly sets upon us, ravisheth our senses, lulls our souls asleep, puffs up our hearts as so many bladders, and that without all feeling, in so much as *those that re misaffected with it, never so much as once perceive it, or think of any cure.* We commonly love him best in this malady, that doth us most harm, and are very willing to be hurt; we gladly listen to flattery, (saith Jerome) we love him, we love him, for it: O Bonciarus, such praise from you! 'twas sweet to hear it. And, as Pliny doth ingeniously confess to his dear friend Augurinus, *all thy writings are most acceptable, but those especially that speak of us.* Again, a little after to Maximus: *I cannot express how pleasing it is to me to hear myself commended.*

Our obscurity

Of so many myriads of Poets, Rhetoricians, Philosophers, Sophisters, as Eusebius well observes, which have written in former ages, scarce one of a thousand's works remains, their books and bodies are perished together. It is not as they vainly think, they shall surely be admired and immortal, as one told Philip of Macedon, insulting after a victory, that his shadow was no longer than before, we may say to them,

We marvel too, not as the vulgar we,
But as the Gorgons, Harpies, or Furies see;
  – Buchanan

or if we do applaud, honour and admire; how small a part, in respect of the whole world, never so much as hears our names! how few take notice of us! how slender a tract, as scant as Alcibiades his land in a Map! And yet every man must and will be immortal, as he hopes, and extend his fame to our Antipodes, when as half, no not a quarter, of his own Province or City, neither knows nor hears of him: but say they did, what's a City to a Kingdom, a Kingdom to Europe, Europe to the World, the World itself that must have an end, if compared to the least visible Star in the Firmament, eighteen times bigger than it? And then if those Stars be infinite, and every Star there be a Sun, as some will, and as this Sun of ours hath his Planets about him, all inhabited, what proportion bear we to them, and where's our glory? As he crackt in Petronius, all the world was under Augustus: and so in Constantine's time, Eusebius brags he governed all the world, so of Alexander it is given out, the four Monarchies, etc., when as neither Greeks nor Romans ever had the fifteenth part of the now known world, nor half of that which was then described. What braggadocians are they and we then! as he said, the name of glory shall be despised, how short a time, how little a while, doth this fame of ours continue! Every private Province, every small Territory and City, when we have all done, will yield as generous spirits, as brave examples, in all respects as famous as ourselves! Cadwallader in Wales, Rollo in Normandy, Robin Hood and Little John as much renowned in Sherwood, as Cæsar in Rome, Alexander in Greece or his Hephæstio. In all ages and among all people, every Town, City, Book, is full of brave Soldiers, Senators, Scholars, and though Brasidas was a worthy Captain, a good man, and, as they thought, not to be matched in Lacedæmon, yet, as his mother truly said, Sparta had many better men than ever he was; and howsoever thou admires thyself, thy friend, many an obscure fellow the world never took notice of, had he been in place or action, would have done much better than he or he, or thou thyself.

Another kind of mad men there is, opposite to these, that are insensibly mad, and know not of it, such as contemn all praise and glory, think themselves most free, when as indeed they are most mad: they trample upon others, but with a different kind of pride: a company of Cynicks, such as are Monks, Hermits, Anachorites, that contemn the world, contemn themselves, contemn all titles, honours, offices: and yet in that contempt are more proud than any man living whatsoever. They are proud in humility, proud in that they are not proud; with a greater vanity, oftimes, does a man glory of his contempt of vain glory, as Austin hath it, like Diogenes, they brag inwardly, and feed themselves fat with a self-conceit of sanctity, which is no better than hypocrisy. They go in sheep's russet, many great men that might maintain themselves in cloth of gold, and seem to be dejected, humble, by their outward carriage, when as inwardly they are swoln full of pride, arrogancy, and self-conceit.

The miseries of scholars

Two main reasons may be given of it, why students should be more subject to this malady than others. The one is, they live a sedentary, solitary life, to themselves and letters, free from bodily exercise, and those ordinary disports which other men use: and many times, if discontent and idleness concur with it, which is too frequent, they are precipitated into this gulf on a sudden: but the common cause is overmuch study; too much learning (as Festus told Paul) hath made thee mad. […][H]ard students are commonly troubled with gouts, catarrhs, rheums, wasting, indigestion, bad eyes, stone and colick, crudities, oppilations, *vertigo*, winds, consumptions and all such diseases as come by overmuch sitting; they are most part lean, dry, ill coloured, spend their fortunes, lose their wits, and many times their lives, and all through immoderate pains and extraordinary studies. […] Because they cannot ride a horse, which every clown can do; salute and court a gentlewoman, carve at table, cringe, and make congies, which every common swasher can do, etc., they are laughed to scorn, and accounted silly fools by our gallants. Yea, many times, such is their misery, they deserve it: a mere scholar, a mere ass. […] [But if] they be studious, industrious, of ripe wits, and perhaps good capacities, then how many diseases of body and mind must they encounter! No labour in the world like unto study! It may be, their temperature will not endure it, but, striving to be excellent, to know all, they lose health, wealth, wit, life, and all. Let him yet happily escape all these hazards, with a body of brass, and is now consummate and ripe, he hath profited in his studies, and proceeded with all applause: after many expences, he is fit for preferment: where shall he have it? He is as far to seek it (after twenty years' standing) as he was at the first day of his coming to the University. For what course shall he take, being now capable and ready? The most parable* and easy, and about which many are employed, is to teach a School, turn Lecturer or Curate, and for that he shall have a Falconer's wages, ten pounds a year, and his diet, or some small stipend, so long as he can please his Patron or the Parish; if they approve him not (for usually they do but a year or two) as inconstant as they that cried *Hosanna!* one day, and *Crucify him!* the other; serving-man-like, he must go and look [for] a new Master: if they do, what is his reward?

> *This too awaits: your fate may be to teach*
> *In some suburban school the parts of speech*
> *– Horace*

Like an ass, he wears out his time for provender†, and can shew a stump rod, saith Hædus, an old torn gown, an ensign of his infelicity, he hath his labour for his pain, a *modicum* to keep him till he be decrepit, and that is all. The scholar is not a happy man. If he be a trencher Chaplain in a Gentleman's house, as it befell Euphormio, after some seven years' service, he may perchance have a Living to the halves, or some small Rectory with the mother of the maids at length, a poor kinswoman, or a crackt chambermaid, to have and to hold during the time of his life. But if he offend his good Patron, or displease his Lady Mistress in the mean time, as Hercules did by Cacus, he shall be dragged forth of doors by the heels, away with him! If he bend his forces to some other studies, with an intent to be secretary to some Nobleman,

* Procurable
† Fodder

or in such a place with an Ambassador, he shall find that these persons rise like Prentices one under another, as in so many Tradesmen's shops, when the Master is dead, the Foreman of the shop commonly steps in his place. Now for Poets, Rhetoricians, Historians, Philosophers, Mathematicians, Sophisters, etc., they are like Grasshoppers, sing they must in Summer, and pine in the Winter, for there is no preferment for them.

Bad education

Parents and such as have the tuition and oversight of children, offend many times in that they are too stern, always threatening, chiding, brawling, whipping, or striking; by means of which their poor children are so disheartened and cowed, that they never after have any courage, a merry hour in their lives, or take pleasure in any thing. There is a great moderation to be had in such things, as matters of so great moment to the making or marring of a child. Some fright their children with beggars, bugbears, and hobgoblins, if they cry, or be otherwise unruly: but they are much to blame in it, many times, saith Lavater, for fear they fall into many diseases, and cry out in their sleep, and are much the worse for it all their lives: these things ought not at all, or to be sparingly done, and upon just occasion. Tyrannical, impatient, hare-brain Schoolmasters, dry-as-dusts, so Fabius terms them, flogging Ajaxes, are in this kind as bad as hangmen and executioners, they make many children endure a martyrdom all the while they are at school, with bad diet, if they board in their houses, too much severity and ill usage, they quite pervert their temperature of body and mind: still chiding, railing, frowning, lashing, tasking, keeping, that they are broken in spirit, moped many times, weary of their lives, and think no slavery in the world (as once I did myself) like to that of a Grammar Scholar.

Loss of liberty

To this catalogue of causes I may well annex loss of liberty, servitude, or imprisonment, which to some persons is as great a

torture as any of the rest. Though they have all things convenient, sumptuous houses to their use, fair walks and gardens, deli-
cious bowers, galleries, good fare and diet, and all things
correspondent, yet they are not content, because they are
confined, may not come and go at their pleasure, have and do
what they will, but live at another man's table and command. As
it is in meats, so is it in all other things, places, societies, sports;
let them be never so pleasant, commodious, wholesome, so good;
yet there is a loathing satiety of all things (the children of Israel
were tired with *Manna*); it is irksome to them so to live, as to a
bird in a cage, or a dog in his kennel, they are weary of it. They
are happy, it is true, and have all things, to another man's judgment, that heart can wish, or that they themselves can desire, had
they but sense of their blessings, yet they loathe it, and are tired
with the present. Men's nature is still desirous of news, variety,
delights; and our wandering affections are so irregular in this
kind, that they must change, though it be to the worst. Bachelors
must be married, and married men would be bachelors; they do
not love their own wives, though otherwise fair, wise, virtuous,
and well qualified, because they are theirs; our present estate is
still the worst; we cannot endure one course of life long (and hate
what we have just prayed for) one calling long, to be in office
pleases, then, in a twinkling, displeases, one place long – at Rome
I long for Tibur, and at Tibur long for Rome; that which we
earnestly sought, we now contemn. This alone kills many a man,
that they are tied to the same still; as a horse in a mill, a dog in
a wheel, they run round, without alteration or news; their life
groweth odious, the world loathsome, and that which crosseth
their furious delights, *What? still the same?*

Poverty
Poverty and want are so violent oppugners*, so unwelcome
guests, so much abhorred of all men, that I may not omit to

* Attackers

speak of them apart. Poverty, although (if considered aright, to a wise, understanding, truly regenerate and contented man) it be a blessed estate, the way to Heaven, as Chrysostom calls it, God's gift, the mother of modesty and much to be preferred before riches (as shall be shewed in his place) yet, as it is esteemed in the world's censure, it is a most odious calling, vile and base, a severe torture, a most intolerable burden. We shun it all, worse than a dog or a snake, we abhor the name of it, poverty is shunned and persecuted throughout the world as being the fountain of all other miseries, cares, woes, labours, and grievances whatsoever. To avoid which, we will take any pains, – hasten to India's furthest bounds, we will leave no haven, no coast, no creek of the world unsearched, though it be to the hazard of our lives; we will dive to the bottom of the sea, to the bowels of the earth, five, six, seven, eight, nine hundred fathom deep, through all five Zones, and both extremes of heat and cold: we will turn parasites and slaves, prostitute ourselves, swear and lie, damn our bodies and souls, forsake God, abjure Religion, steal, rob, murder, rather than endure this unsufferable yoke of Poverty, which doth so tyrannize, crucify, and generally depress us. [...] Which is most grievous, poverty makes men ridiculous, they must endure jests, taunts, flouts, blows, of their betters, and take all in good part to get a meal's meat: poverty is a great reproach, bids us do and suffer all. He must turn parasite, jester, fool (to play with folly, saith Euripides), slave, villain, drudge, to get a poor living, apply himself to each man's humours, to win and please, etc. and be buffeted, when he hath all done, (as Ulysses was by Melanthius in Homer), be reviled, baffled, insulted over, for the folly of the powerful must be endured, and may not so much as mutter against it. He must turn rogue and villain, for, as the saying is, poverty alone makes men thieves, rebels, murderers, traitors, assassinates [assassins], (because of poverty we have sinned,) swear and forswear, bear false witness, lie, dissemble, any thing, as I say, to advantage themselves, and to relieve their necessities; it instigates to crime, when a man is driven to his shifts, what will he not do?

If cruel fortune has made Sinon wretched,
'Twill also make of him a faithless liar;
  – Virgil

he will betray his father, Prince, and Country, turn Turk, forsake Religion, abjure God and all; there is no treason so horrible (saith Leo Afer) that they will not commit for gain. Plato therefore calls poverty *thievish, sacrilegious, filthy, wicked and mischievous*, and well he might; for it makes many an upright man otherwise, had he not been in want, to take bribes, to be corrupt, to do against his conscience, to sell his tongue, heart, hand, etc., to be churlish, hard, unmerciful, uncivil, to use indirect means to help his present estate. It makes Princes to exact upon their subjects, Great men tyrannize, Landlords oppress, Justices mercenary, Lawyers vultures, Physicians Harpies, friends importunate, tradesmen liars, honest men thieves, devout assassinates, great men to prostitute their wives, daughters, and themselves, middle sort to repine, commons to mutiny, all to grudge, murmur and complain. A great temptation to all mischief, it compels some miserable wretches to counterfeit several diseases, to dismember, make themselves blind, lame, to have a more plausible cause to beg, and lose their limbs and to recover their present wants. Jodocus Damhoderius, a Lawyer of Bruges, hath some notable examples of such counterfeit cranks, and every village almost will yield abundant testimonies amongst us; we have dummerers*, *Abraham* men[†]; etc.. And, that which is the extent of misery, it enforceth them, through anguish and wearisomeness of their lives, to make away themselves. They had rather be hanged, drowned, etc. than to live without means.

---

* Those who feign dumbness
[†] Beggars feigning lunacy

Loss of friends

In this Labyrinth of accidental causes, the farther I wander, the more intricate I find the passage, and new causes as so many by-paths offer themselves to be discussed. To search out all were an Herculean work, and fitter for Theseus: I will follow mine intended thread; and point only at some few of the chiefest.

Amongst which loss and death of friends may challenge a first place. As Vives well observes, many are melancholy after a feast, holy-day, merry meeting, or some pleasing sport, if they be solitary by chance, left alone to themselves, without employment, sport, or want their ordinary companions; some, at the departure of friends only, whom they shall shortly see again, weep and howl, and look after them as a cow lows after her calf, or a child takes on that goes to school after holidays. Thy coming (which Tully writ to Atticus), was not so welcome to me as thy departure was harsh. Montanus makes mention of a country woman that, parting with her friends and native place, became grievously melancholy for many years; and Trallianus of another, so caused for the absence of her husband. Which is an ordinary passion amongst our good wives; if their husband tarry out a day longer than his appointed time, or break his hour, they take on presently with sighs and tears, 'he is either robbed dead, some mischance or other is surely befallen him,' they cannot eat, drink, sleep, or be quiet in mind, till they see him again. If parting of friends, absence alone, can work such violent effects, what shall death do, when they must eternally be separated, never in this world to meet again? This is so grievous a torment for the time, that it takes away their appetite, desire of life, extinguisheth all delights, it causeth deep sighs and groans, tears, exclamations,

O mother's sweet child! O my very blood
O tender flower! alas! and art thou gone?

howling, roaring, many bitter pangs, and by frequent meditation extends so far sometimes, *they think they see their dead friends continually in their eyes*, as Conciliator confesseth he saw his mother's ghost presenting herself before him. What the wretched overmuch desire, they easily believe; still, still, still, that good father, that good son, that good wife, that dear friend runs in their minds; a single thought fills all their mind all the year long.

Futile philosophy

What is most of our Philosophy, but a labyrinth of opinions, idle questions, propositions, metaphysical terms? Socrates held all Philosophers cavillers and mad men, saith Eusebius, because they commonly sought after such things which could be neither understood nor grasped by us, or, put case they did understand, yet they were altogether unprofitable. For what matter is it for us to know how high the *Pleiades* are, how far distant *Perseus* and *Cassiopea* from us, how deep the sea, etc.? We are neither wiser, as he follows it, nor modester, not better nor richer, nor stronger, for the knowledge of it. What is above us does not concern us. I may say the same of those Genethliacal* studies. What is Astrology, but vain elections, predictions?; all Magick, but a troublesome error, a pernicious foppery? Physick, but intricate rules and prescriptions? Philology, but vain criticisms? Logick, [but] needless sophisms? Metaphysicks themselves, but intricate subtilties, and fruitless abstractions? Alchemy, but a bundle of errors? To what end are such great Tomes? why do we spend so many years in their studies? Much better to know nothing at all, as those barbarous Indians are wholly ignorant, than, as some of us, to be so sore vexed about unprofitable toys, it is foolish to waste labour on trifles, to build an house without pins, make a rope of sand; to what end? for whose benefit? He studies on, but, as the boy told St. Austin, when I have laved the sea dry, thou shalt understand the mystery of Trinity. He makes observations, keeps times and seasons; and as Conradus the Emperor would not touch his new Bride, till an Astrologer had told him a mascu-

* Nativity-related

line hour; but with what success? He travels into Europe, Africa, Asia, searcheth every creek, sea, city, mountain, gulf; to what end? See one promontory, saith Socrates of old, one mountain, one sea, one river, and see all. [...] We run, ride, take indefatigable pains, all up early, down late, striving to get that which we had better be without; [...] it were much fitter for us to be quiet, sit still, and take our ease.

The outward symptoms of melancholy

Hippocrates, in his book On Insanity and Melancholy, reckons up these signs, that they are *lean, withered, hollow-eyed, look old, wrinkled, harsh, much troubled with wind, and a griping in their bellies, or belly-ache, belch often, dry bellies and hard, dejected looks, flaggy beards, singing of the ears, vertigo, lightheaded, little or no sleep, and that interrupt, terrible and fearful dreams,* – Sister Anne, what dreams be these that confound and appal me! The same symptoms are repeated by Melanelius (in his Book of Melancholy, collected out of Galen, Ruffus, Aëtius,) by Rhasis, Gordonius, and all the Juniors, *continual, sharp and stinking belchings, as if the meat in their stomack were putrefied, or that they had eaten fish, dry bellies, absurd and interrupt dreams, and many phantastical visions about their eyes, vertiginous, apt to tremble, and prone to Venery.* Some add palpitation of the heart, cold sweat, as usual symptoms, and a leaping in many parts of the body, a kind of itching, saith Laurentius, on the superfices of the skin, like a flea-biting sometimes. Montaltus puts fixed eyes and much twinkling of their eyes for a sign; and so doth Avicenna, they are very red-faced, etc.; they stutter most part, which he took out of Hippocrates' Aphorisms. Rhasis makes *headache and a binding heaviness* for a principal token, *much leaping of wind about the skin, as well as stutting, or tripping in speech, etc., hollow eyes, gross veins and broad lips.* To some too, if they be far gone, mimical gestures are too familiar, laughing, grinning, fleering*, murmuring, talking to themselves,

* Mocking

with strange mouths and faces, inarticulate voices, exclamations, etc.. And although they be commonly lean, hirsute, uncheerful in countenance, withered, and not so pleasant to behold, by reason of those continual fears, griefs, and vexations, dull, heavy, lazy, restless, unapt to go about any business: yet their memories are most part good, they have happy wits, and excellent apprehensions. Their hot and dry brains make them they cannot sleep, they have mighty and often watchings, sometimes waking for a month, a year, together.

Irrational fears

Some are afraid that heaven will fall on their heads: some afraid they are damned, or shall be. *They are troubled with scruples of Conscience, distrusting God's mercies, think they shall go certainly to Hell, the Devil will have them, and make great lamentation,* Jason Pratensis. Fear of Devils, death, that they shall be sick of some such or such disease, ready to tremble at every object, they shall die themselves forthwith, or that some of their dear friends or near allies are certainly dead; imminent danger, loss, disgrace, still torment others, etc. that they are all glass, and therefore they will suffer no man to come near them; that they are all cork, as light as feathers; others as heavy as lead; some are afraid their heads will fall off their shoulders, that they have frogs in their bellies, etc.. Montanus speaks of one *that durst not walk alone from home, for fear he should swoon, or die.* A second *fears every man he meets will rob him, quarrel with him, or kill him.* A third dares not venture to walk alone, for fear he should meet the Devil, a thief, be sick, fears all old women as witches, and every black dog or cat he sees he suspecteth to be a Devil, every person comes near him is maleficiated [bewitched], every creature, all intend to hurt him, seek his ruin. Another dares not go over a bridge, come near a pool, rock, steep hill, lie in a chamber where cross beams are, for fear he be tempted to hang, drown, or precipitate himself. If he be in a silent auditory, as at a sermon, he is afraid he shall speak aloud at unawares, some thing undecent, unfit to be said. If he be locked in a close room, he is afraid of being stifled for want of air, and still carries biscuit, Aquavitae, or some strong waters about him, for fear of fainting, or being sick; or if he be in a throng, middle of a Church, multitude, where he may not well get out, though he sit at ease, he is so misaffected. He will freely promise, undertake any business beforehand, but, when it comes to be performed, he dare not adventure, but fears an infinite number of dangers, disasters, etc.. Some are *afraid to be burned, or that the ground will sink under them, or swallow them quick, or that the King will call them in question for some fact they never did, and that they shall surely be executed.* The terror of such a death troubles them, and they fear as much, and are equally tormented in mind, *as they that have committed a murder, and are pensive without a cause, as if they were now presently to be put to death.* They are afraid of some loss, danger, that they shall surely lose their lives, goods, and all they have, but why they know not.

Obsessions

If they see a stage-play, they run upon that a week after; if they hear music, or see dancing, they have nought but bag-pipes in their brain; if they see a combat, they are all for arms; if abused, an abuse troubles them long after; if crossed, that cross, etc.. Restless in their thoughts and actions, continually meditating, more like dreams than men awake, they feign a company of antick, phantastical conceits, they have most frivolous thoughts, impossible to be effected; and sometimes think verily they hear and see present before their eyes such phantasms or goblins, they fear, suspect, or conceive, they still talk with, and follow them. In fine, their thoughts are like to dreams; still, saith Avicenna, they wake as others dream, and such for the most part are their imaginations and conceits, absurd, vain, foolish toys, yet they are most curious and solicitous; continually beyond all bounds and preoccupied with something or other; as serious in a toy, as if it were a most necessary business, of great moment, importance, and still, still, still, thinking of it, macerating themselves. Though they do talk with you, and seem to be otherwise employed, and to your thinking very intent and busy, still that toy runs in their mind, that fear, that suspicion, that abuse, that jealousy, that agony, that vexation, that cross, that castle in the air, that crotchet, that whimsy, that fiction, that pleasant waking dream, whatsoever it is. They neither ask questions nor respond to them, (saith Fracastorius); they do not much heed what you say, their mind is on another matter; ask what you will, they do not attend, or much intend that business they are about, but forget themselves what they are saying, doing, or should otherwise say or do, whither they are going, distracted with their own melancholy thoughts. One laughs upon a sudden, another smiles to himself, a third frowns, calls, his lips go still, he acts with his hand, as he walks, etc. 'Tis proper to all melancholy men, saith Mercurialis, *what conceit they have once entertained, to be most intent, violent, and continually about it.* It happens, willy-nilly, do what they may, they cannot be rid of it, against their wills they must think of it a thousand times over, they are continually troubled with it, in company, out of company; at meat, at exercise, at all times and places, they do not cease to think about what they least wish to remember; if it be offensive especially, they cannot forget it, they may not rest or sleep for it, but, still tormenting themselves, they roll upon themselves the stone of Sisyphus, as Brunner observes. It is a perpetual calamity, and terrible scourge.

The Chaos of Melancholy

The Tower of *Babel* never yielded such confusion of tongues, as this Chaos of Melancholy doth variety of symptoms. There is in all melancholy, like men's faces, a disagreeing likeness still; and as, in a river, we swim in the same place, though not in the same numerical water; as the same instrument affords several lessons, so the same disease yields diversity of symptoms.

Melancholy adust, or the burning of the four humours*

[T]he most immediate symptoms[†] proceed from […] distemperature of spirits (which, as Hercules de Saxonia contends, are wholly immaterial), or from the four humours in those seats, whether they be hot or cold, natural, unnatural, innate or adventitious, intended or remitted, simple or mixt, their diverse mixtures, and several adustions, combinations, which may be as diversely varied as those first four qualities in Clavius, and produce as many several symptoms and monstrous fictions as wine doth effects, which, as Andreas Bachius observes, are infinite. Of greater note be these.

If it be natural Melancholy, as Lod. Mercatus, T. Bright, hath largely described, either of the Spleen, or of the veins, faulty by excess of quantity, or thickness of substance, it is a cold and dry humour, as Montanus affirms, the parties are sad, timorous, and fearful. Prosper Calenus, in his book, will have them to be more stupid than ordinary, cold, heavy, dull, solitary, sluggish, if they have much black and cold bile. Hercules de Saxonia *holds these that are naturally melancholy to be of a leaden colour or black*, and so doth Guianerius, and such as think themselves dead many times, or that they see, talk with, black men, dead men, Spirits and Goblins frequently, if it be in excess. These symptoms vary according to the mixture of those four humours adust, which is unnatural melancholy. For, as Trallianus hath written, *there is not one cause of this melancholy, nor one humour which begets it, but divers diversely intermixt, from whence proceeds this variety of symptoms:* and those varying again as they are hot or cold. *Cold melancholy* (saith Benedic. Vittorius Faventinus), *is a cause of dotage, and*

---

*A technical passage. Burton describes how melancholy 'adust' – or burnt melancholy – could be produced in the body by burning any of the four humours. Burnt melancholy itself could produce melancholy adust, but so could burnt blood, phlegm or choler. Each of these adustions, by burning a person's dominant humour and so upsetting the balance of their natural temperament, could cause different symptoms of melancholy madness.
[†] Of melancholy

more mild symptoms; if hot or more adust, of more violent passions and furies. Fracastorius will have us to consider well of it, *with what kind of Melancholy every one is troubled, for it much avails to know it; one is enraged by fervent heat, another is possessed by sad and cold; one is fearful, shamefast, the other impudent and bold,* as Ajax, who furiously snatched up arms and demanded battle – quite mad or tending to madness: attacking now this, now that. Bellerophon, on the other side, wanders alone in the woods; one despairs, weeps, is weary of his life, another laughs etc.. All which variety is produced from the several degrees of that and cold, which Hercules de Saxonia will have wholly proceed from the distemperature of spirits alone, animal especially, and those immaterial, the next, and immediate causes of Melancholy, as they are hot, cold, dry, moist, and from their agitation proceeds that diversity of symptoms, which he reckons up in the 13th chap. of his Tract of Melancholy, and that largely through every part. Others will have them come from the diverse adustion of the four humours, which, in this unnatural melancholy, by corruption of blood, adust choler, or melancholy natural, *by excessive distemper of that turned, in comparison of the natural, into a sharp lye by force of adustion, cause, according to the diversity of their matter, diverse and strange symptoms,* which T. Bright reckons up in his following chapter. So doth Arculanus, according to the four principal humours adust, and many others.

For example, if it proceed from phlegm, (which is seldom and not so frequent as the rest), it stirs up dull symptoms, and a kind of stupidity, or impassionate hurt: they are sleepy, saith Savanarola, dull, slow, cold, blockish, ass-like; asinine melancholy, Melancthon calls it: *they are much given to weeping, and delight in waters, ponds, pools, rivers, fishing, fowling, etc.* they are pale of colour, slothful, apt to sleep, heavy: much troubled with head-ache, continual meditation, and muttering to themselves; they dream of waters, that they are in danger of drowning, and fear such things, Rhasis. They are fatter than others that are melancholy, of a muddy complexion, apter to spit, sleep, more troubled with rheum than the rest, and have their eyes still fixed on the ground. Such a patient had Hercules de Saxonia, a widow in Venice, that was fat and very sleepy still; Christophorus à Vega another affected in the same sort. If it be inveterate or violent, the symptoms are more evident, they plainly dote, and are ridiculous to others, in all their gestures, actions, speeches: imagining impossibilities, as he in Christophorus à Vega, that thought he was a Tun of Wine, and that Siennois, that resolved with himself not to piss, for fear he should drown all the town.

If it proceed from blood adust, or that there be a mixture of blood in it, *such are commonly ruddy of complexion, and high-coloured*, according to Sallustius Salvianus, and Hercules de Saxonia; and, as Savanarola, Vittorius Faventinus, farther add, *the veins of their eyes be red, as well as their faces.* They are much inclined to laughter, witty and merry, conceited in discourse, pleasant, if they be not far gone, much given to musick, dancing, and to be in women's company. They meditate wholly on such things, and think *they see or hear plays, dancing, and such like sports* (free from all fear and sorrow, as Hercules de Saxonia supposeth,) if they be more strongly possessed with his kind of melancholy. Arnoldus adds, like him of Argos in the Poet, that sat laughing all day long, as if he had been at a Theatre. Such another is mentioned by Aristotle, living at Abydos, a town of Asia Minor, that would sit after the same fashion, as if he had been upon a Stage, and sometimes act himself; now clap his hands, and laugh, as if he had been well pleased with the sight. Wolfius relates of a country fellow called Brunsellius, subject to this humour, *that, being by chance at a sermon, saw a woman fall off from a form half asleep, at which object most of the company laughed, but he, for his part, was so much moved, that for three whole days after he did nothing but laugh, by which means he was much weakened, and worse a long time following.* Such a one was old Sophocles, and Democritus himself had a merry kind of madness, much in this vein. Laurentius thinks this kind of melancholy, which is a little adust with some mixture of blood, to be that which Aristotle meant, when he said melancholy men of all others are most witty, which causeth many times divine ravishment, and a kind of divine inspiration, which stirreth them up to be excellent Philosophers, Poets, Prophets, etc.. Mercurialis gives instance in a young man his patient, sanguine melancholy, *of a great wit, and excellently learned.*

If it arise from choler adust, they are bold and impudent, and of a more harebrain disposition, apt to quarrel and think of such things, battles, combats, and their manhood; furious, impatient in discourse, stiff, irrefragable, and prodigious in their tenet; and, if they be moved, most violent, outrageous, ready to disgrace, provoke any, to kill themselves and others; Arnoldus adds, stark mad by fits, *they sleep little, their urine is subtile and fiery; (Guianerius) in their fits you shall hear them speak all manner of languages, Hebrew, Greek and Latin, that never were taught or knew them before.* Apponensis speaks of a mad woman that spake excellent good Latin; and Rhasis knew another, that could prophecy in her fit, and foretell things truly to come. Guianerius had a patient could make Latin verses when the Moon was combust*, otherwise illiterate. Avicenna and some of his adherents will have these symptoms, when they happen, to proceed from the Devil, and that they are rather possessed, than mad or melancholy, or both together, as Jason Pratensis thinks, but most ascribe it to the humour. [...] Cardan holds these men of all others fit to be assassinates, bold, hardy, fierce, and adventurous, to undertake any thing by reason of their choler adust. *This humour,* saith he, *prepares them to endure death itself, and all manner of torments, with invincible courage, and 'tis a wonder to see with what alacrity they will undergo such tortures,* that it seems preternatural: he ascribes this generosity, fury, or rather stupidity, to this adustion of choler and melancholy: but I take these rather to be mad or desperate, than properly melancholy: for commonly this humour, so adust and hot, degenerates into madness.

* Obscured by the sun

If it come from melancholy itself adust, those men, saith *Avicenna, are usually sad and solitary, and that continually, and in excess, more than ordinary suspicious, more fearful, and have long, sore, and most corrupt imaginations*; cold and black, bashful and so solitary, that, as Arnoldus writes, *they will endure no company, they dream of graves still, and dead men, and think themselves bewitched or dead*: if it be extreme, they think they hear hideous noises, see and talk *with black men, and converse familiarly with Devils, and such strange chimaeras and visions*, (Gordonius), or that they are possessed by them, that somebody talks to them, or within them. Such melancholy folk are generally possessed. Valescus de Taranta had such a woman in cure, *that thought she had to do with the Devil*: and Gentilus Fulgosus writes that he had a melancholy friend, that *had a black man in the likeness of a soldier*, still following him wheresoever he was. Laurentius hath many stories of such as have thought themselves bewitched by their enemies; and some that would eat no meat as being dead. In the year 1550, an Advocate of Paris fell into such a melancholy fit, that he believed verily he was dead; he could not be persuaded otherwise, or to eat or drink, till a kinsman of his, a Scholar of Bourges, did eat before him, dressed like a corse. The story, saith Serre, was acted in a Comedy before Charles the Ninth. Some think they are beasts, wolves, hogs, and cry like dogs, foxes, bray like asses, and low like kine, as King Proeteus' daughters, Hildesheim hath an example of a Dutch Baron so affected, and Trincavellius another of a nobleman in his country, *that thought he was certainly a beast, and would imitate most of their voices*, with many such symptoms, which may properly be reduced to this kind. […]

Who can speak sufficiently of these symptoms, or prescribe rules to comprehend them? […] They are irregular, obscure, various, so infinite, Proteus himself is not so diverse; you may as well make the Moon a new coat, as a true character of a melancholy man; as soon find the motion of a bird in the air, as the heart of man, a melancholy man.

Melancholy of maids and widows

[S]eldom shall you see an hired servant, a poor hand maid, though ancient, that is kept hard to her work and bodily labour, a coarse country wench, troubled in this kind*, but Noble Virgins, nice Gentlewomen, such as are solitary and idle, live at ease, lead a life out of action and employment, that fare well, in great houses and jovial companies, ill-disposed peradventure of themselves, and not willing to make any resistance, discontented otherwise, of weak judgement, able bodies, and subject to passions; noble maids, saith Mercatus, barren women, and widows, are generally melancholy, such for the most part are misaffected, and prone to this disease. I do not so much pity them that may otherwise be eased, but those alone that out of a strong temperament, innate constitution, are violently carried away with this torrent of inward humours, and though very modest of themselves, sober, religious, virtuous, and well given, (as many so distressed maids are), yet cannot make resistance; these grievances will appear, this malady will take place, and now manifestly shews itself, and may not otherwise be helped. But where am I? Into what subject have I rushed? What have I to do with Nuns, Maids, Virgins, Widows? I am a Bachelor myself, and lead a Monastick life in a College. I am truly a very unfit person to talk about these subjects, I confess 'tis an *indecorum* and as Pallas, a Virgin, blushed, when Jupiter by chance spoke of Love matters in her presence, and turned away her face, I will check myself; though my subject necessarily require it, I will say no more.

And yet I will and must say something more, add a word or two on behalf of Maids and Widows, in favour of all such distressed parties, in commiseration of their present estate. And as I cannot choose but condole their mishap that labour of this infirmity, and are destitute of help in this case, so must I need inveigh against them that are in fault, more than manifest causes, and as bitterly tax those tyrannizing pseudo-politicians' superstitious orders, rash vows, hard-hearted parents, guardians, unnatural friends, allies

* i.e. melancholy

(call them how you will), those careless and stupid overseers, that, out of worldly respects, covetousness, supine negligence, their own private ends, (because, meanwhile, it is well for him), can so severely reject, stubbornly neglect, and impiously contemn without all remorse and pity, the tears, sighs, groans, and grievous miseries, of such poor souls committed to their charge. How odious and abominable are those superstitious and rash vows of Popish Monasteries, so to bind and enforce men and women to vow virginity, to lead a single life against the laws of nature, opposite to religion, policy, and humanity, so to starve, to offer violence to, to suppress the vigour of youth! by rigorous statutes, severe laws, vain persuasions, to debar them of that to which by their innate temperature they are so furiously inclined, urgently carried, and sometimes precipitated, even irresistibly led, to the prejudice of their souls' heath, and good state of body and mind! and all for base and private respects, to maintain their gross superstition, to enrich themselves and their territories, as they falsely suppose, by hindering some marriages, that the world be not full of beggars, and their parishes pestered with orphans! [...] It troubles me to think of, much more to relate, those frequent aborts and murdering of infants in their Nunneries, (read Kemnitius and others), their notorious fornications, those male-prostitutes, masturbators, strumpets, etc., those rapes, incests, adulteries, mastuprations*, sodomies, buggeries, of Monks and Friars. See Bale's Visitation of Abbies, Mercurialis, Rodericus à Castro, Pete Forestus, and divers physicians. I know their ordinary apologies and excuses for these things, but let the Politicians†, the Doctors, and Theologians look out: I shall more opportunely meet them elsewhere.

> *Lest you should think that I do plead*
> *Some certain maid's or widow's need,*
> *I'll say no more.*

* Masturbations
† Political writers

The Second Partition

Burton considers a range of cures for melancholy and pursues some long digressions.

Inveterate Melancholy, howsoever it may seem to be a continuate, inexorable disease, hard to be cured, accompanying them to their graves most part, as Montanus observes, yet many times it may be helped, even that which is most violent, or at least, according to the same Author, it may be mitigated and much eased. Never despair. It may be hard to cure, but not impossible, for him that is most grievously affected, if he be but willing to be helped.

Upon this good hope I will proceed, using the same method in the cure, which I have formerly used in the rehearsing of the causes; first *general*, then *particular*; and those according to their several species. Of these cures some be *lawful*, some again *unlawful*, which, though frequent, familiar, and often used, yet justly censured, and to be controverted. As first, whether by these diabolical means, which are commonly practised by the Devil and his Ministers, Sorcerers, Witches, Magicians, etc., by Spells, Cabalistical words, Charms, Characters, Images, Amulets, Ligatures, Philters, Incantations, etc., this disease and the like may be cured? and if they may, whether it be lawful to make use of them? […] 'Tis a common practice of some men to go to a Witch, and then to a Physician; if one cannot, the other shall; if they cannot bend Heaven, they will try Hell. It matters not, saith Paracelsus, whether it be God or the Devil, Angels or unclean Spirits cure him, so that he be eased. If a man fall into a ditch, as he prosecutes it, what matter is it whether a friend or an enemy help him out? and if I be troubled with such a malady, what care I whether the Devil himself, or any of his Ministers, by God's permission, redeem me?

A digression of the air

As a long-winged Hawk, when he is first whistled off the fist, mounts aloft, and for his pleasure fetcheth many a circuit in the Air, still soaring higher and higher, till he be come to his full pitch, and in the end, when the game is sprung, comes down amain, and stoops upon a sudden: so will I, having now come at last into these ample fields of Air, wherein I may freely expatiate and exercise myself for my recreation, a while rove, wander round about the world, mount aloft to those ethereal orbs and celestial spheres, and so descend to my former elements again.

Bird migration

I would find out with Trajan the Fountains of the Danube, of Ganges, Oxus, see those Egyptian Pyramids, Trajan's Bridge, the Grotto of the Sibyls, Lucullus' Fish-ponds, the Temple of Nidrose, etc., and, if I could, observe what becomes of swallows, storks, cranes, cuckoos, nightingales, redstarts, and many other kind of singing birds, water-fowls, hawks, etc. some of them are only seen in summer, some in winter; some are observed in the snow, and at no other times, each have their seasons. In winter not a bird is in Muscovy to be found, but at the spring in an instant the woods and hedges are full of them, saith Herbastein: how comes it to pass? Do they sleep in winter, like Gesner's Alpine mice; or do they lie hid (as Olaus affirms) in the bottom of lakes and rivers, holding their breath? often so found by fishermen in Poland and Scandia, two together, mouth to mouth, wing to wing; and when the spring comes they revive again, or if they be brought into a stove, or to the fire side. Or do they follow the Sun, as Peter Martyr manifestly convicts, out of his own knowledge? for, when he was Embassador in Egypt, he saw swallows, Spanish kites, and many such other European birds, in December and January, very familiarly flying, and in great abundance, about Alexandria, where, at that season, the flowers were in bloom and the trees green; or lie they hid in caves, rocks, and hollow trees, as most think, in deep Tin-mines or Sea-cliffs, as Mr Carew gives out?

Fossils and continental drift

I would have a convenient place to go down with Orpheus, Ulysses, Hercules, Lucian's Menippus, at St Patrick's Purgatory, at Triphonius' den, Hecla in Iceland, Ætna in Sicily, to descend and see what is done in the bowels of the earth; do stones and metals grow there still? how come fir trees to be digged out from tops of hills, as in our mosses and marshes all over Europe? How come they to dig up fish bones, shells, beams, iron-works, many fathoms under ground, and anchors in mountains far remote from all seas? In the year 1460, at Berne in Switzerland, 50 fathom deep, a ship was digged out of a mountain, where they got metal ore, in which were 48 carcasses of men, with other merchandise. [...] Came this from earth quakes, or from Noah's flood, as Christians suppose? or is there a vicissitude of Sea and land? as Anaximenes held of old the mountains of Thessaly would become Seas, and Seas again Mountains. The whole world belike should be new moulded, when it seemed good to those all-commanding Powers, and turned inside out, as we do hay-cocks in Harvest, top to bottom, or bottom to top: or as we turn apples to the fire, move the world upon his Centre; that which is under the Poles now, should be translated to the Æquinoctial, and that which is under the Torrid Zone to the Circle Arctick and Antarctick another while, and so be reciprocally warmed by the Sun: or, if the worlds be infinite, and every fixed star a Sun, with his compassing Planets, (as Brunus and Campanella conclude), cast three or four worlds into one.

The variety of species

Why doth Africa breed so many venomous beasts, Ireland none? Athens owls, Crete none? Why hath Daulis and Thebes no swallows (so Pausanias informs us) as well as the rest of Greece, Ithaca no hares, Pontus no asses, Scythia no swine? Whence come this variety of complexions, colours, plants, birds, beasts, metals, peculiar almost to every place? Why so many thousand strange birds and beasts proper to America alone, as Acosta demands? Were they created in the six days, or ever in Noah's Ark? If there, why are they not dispersed and found in other countries?

Other worlds

If our world be small in respect, why may we not suppose a plurality of worlds, those infinite stars visible in the Firmament to be so many Suns, with particular fixt Centres; to have likewise their subordinate Planets, as the Sun hath his dancing still round him? [...] But who shall dwell in these vast bodies, Earths, Worlds, if they be inhabited? rational creatures? as Kepler demands, or have they souls to be saved? or do they inhabit a better part of the World than we do? Are we or they Lords of the World? And how are all things made for man? It is a difficult knot to untie: 'tis hard to determine.

Travel

[P]eregrination charms our senses with such unspeakable and sweet variety, that some count him unhappy that never travelled, a kind of prisoner, and pity his case that from his cradle to his old age beholds the same still; still, still the same, the same: insomuch that Rhasis doth not only commend but enjoin travel, and such variety of objects to a melancholy man, and to lie in diverse Inns, to be drawn into several companies. [...]

[S]ome are especially affected with such objects as be near, to see passengers go by in some great roadway, or boats in a river, to oversee a Fair, a Market place, or out of a pleasant window into some thorough-fare street, to behold a continual concourse, a promiscuous rout, coming and going, or a multitude of spectators at a Theatre, a Mask, or some such like shew. But I rove: the sum is this, that variety of actions, objects, air, places, are excellent good in this infirmity and all others, good for man, good for beast. Constantine the Emperor holds it an only cure for rotten sheep, and any manner of sick cattle. Lælius à Fonte Eugubinus, that great Doctor, at the latter end of many of his consultations (as commonly he doth set down what success his Physick had) in melancholy most especially approves of this above all other remedies whatsoever: Many other things helped, but change of air was that which wrought the cure, and did most good.

Pastimes

Some men's whole delight is to take Tobacco, and drink all day long in a Tavern, or Ale-house, to discourse, sing, jest, roar, talk of a Cock and Bull over a pot, etc.. Or when three or four good companions meet, tell old stories by the fireside, or in the Sun, as old folks usually do, remembering afresh and with pleasure ancient matters, and such like accidents, which happened in their younger years. Others' best pastime is to game, nothing to them so pleasant. [...]

Dancing, Singing, Masking, Mumming, Stage-plays, howsoever they be heavily censured by some severe Catos, yet, if opportunely and soberly used, may justly be approved. 'Tis better to dig than to dance, saith Austin: but what is that if they delight in it? 'No sober person dances.' But in what kind of dance? I know these sports have many oppugners, whole volumes writ against them, when as all they say (if duly considered) is but an Index of Ignorance; and some again, because they are now cold and wayward, past themselves, cavil at all such youthful sports in others, as he did in the Comedy; they think them born gray-beards, etc.. Some out of preposterous zeal object many times trivial arguments, and because of some abuse will quite take away the good use, as if they should forbid wine, because it makes men drunk; but in my judgment they are too stern: *there is a time for all things, a time to mourn, a time to dance; a time to embrace, a time not to embrace, and nothing better than that a man should rejoice in his own works.* For my part, I will subscribe to the King's Declaration, and was ever of that mind, those May-games, Wakes and Whitsun-Ales etc., if they be not unseasonable hours, may justly be permitted. Let them freely feast, sing and dance, have their Puppet-plays, Hobby-horses, Tabers, Crowds, Bag-pipes, etc., play at Ball, and Barley-breaks, and what sports and recreations they like best.

The joy of study

But amongst these exercises, or recreations of the mind within doors, there is none so general, so aptly to be applied to all sorts of men, so fit and proper to expel Idleness and Melancholy, as that of Study. [...] Who is he that is now wholly overcome with idleness, or otherwise involved in a labyrinth of worldly cares, troubles and discontents, that will not be much lightened in his mind by reading of some enticing story, true or feigned, where (as in a glass) he shall observe what our forefathers have done, the beginnings, ruins, falls, periods of Common-wealths, private men's actions displayed to the life, etc.? Plutarch usually calls them the second course and junkets, because they were usually read at Noblemen's Feasts. Who is not earnestlyaffected with a passionate speech, well penned, an elegant Poem, or some pleasing bewitching discourse, like that of Heliodorus, where quiet pleasure blends with mirth? [...] [W]e have thousands of Authors of all sorts, many great Libraries full well furnished, like so many dishes of meat, served out for several palates; and he is a very block that is affected with none of them. Some take an infinite delight to study the very Languages wherein these books are written, Hebrew, Greek, Syriack, Chaldee, Arabick, etc.. Methinks it would well please any man to look upon a Geographical Map, on account of the incredible variety and pleasantness of the subject, and would excite to further steps in knowledge: Chorographical, Topographical Delineations, to behold, as it were, all the remote Provinces, Towns, Cities of the World, and never go forth of the limits of his study, to measure by the scale and compass their extent, distance, examine their site. [...] [S]o great pleasure, such sweet content, there is in study. King James, 1605, when he came to our University of Oxford, and amongst other edifices, now went to view that famous Library, renowned by Sir Thomas Bodley, in imitation of Alexander, at his departure brake out into that noble speech: If I were not a King, I would be an University man; and if it were so that I must be a prisoner, if I might have my wish, I would desire to have no other prison than that Library, and to be chained together with so many good Authors and dead masters. – So sweet is the delight of study, the more learning they have (as he that hath a Dropsy, the more he drinks the thirstier he is), the more they covet to learn, and the last day is the pupil of the former; harsh at first learning is, – 'bitter the roots' – but 'the fruits are sweet', according to that of Isocrates, pleasant at last; the longer they live, the more they are enamoured with the Muses. Heinsius, the Keeper of the Library at Leyden in Holland, was mewed up in it all the year long; and that which to thy thinking should have bred a loathing caused in him a greater liking. I no sooner (saith he) come into the Library, but I bolt the door to me, excluding lust, ambition, avarice, and all such vices, whose nurse is idleness, the mother of ignorance, and Melancholy herself, and in the very lap of eternity, amongst so many divine souls, I take my seat, with so lofty a spirit and sweet content, that I pity all our great ones, and rich men that know not this happiness. – I am not ignorant in the mean time (notwithstanding this which I have said) how barbarously and basely for the most part our ruder Gentry esteem of Libraries and Books, how they neglect and contemn so great a treasure, so inestimable a benefit, as Æsop's cock did the jewel he found in the dunghill, and all through error, ignorance and want of education. And 'tis a wonder withal to observe how much they will vainly cast away in unnecessary expences, (saith Erasmus), what in hawks, hounds, law-suits, vain building, gourmandizing, drinking, sports, plays, pastimes, etc.. If a well minded man to the Muses would sue to some of them for an Exhibition, to the farther maintenance or enlargement of such a work, be it College, Lecture, Library, or whatsoever else may tend to the Advancement of Learning, they are so unwilling, so averse, they had rather see these which are already with such cost and care erected, utterly ruined, demolished, or otherwise employed; for they repine many and grudge at such gifts and revenues so bestowed: and therefore it were in vain, as Erasmus well notes, to solicit or ask any thing of such men, that are likely damn'd to riches, to this purpose. For my part I pity these men, I let them go as they are, in the catalogue of Ignoramus.

Sleep

As waking, that hurts, by all means must be avoided, so sleep, which so much helps, by like ways must be procured, by nature or art, inwards or outward medicines, and be protracted longer than ordinary, if it may be, as being an especial help. It moistens and fattens the body, concocts, and helps digestion, (as we see in dormice, and those Alpine mice that sleep all Winter), which Gesner speaks of, when they are so found sleeping under the snow in dead of Winter, as fat as butter. It expels cares, pacifies the mind, refresheth the weary limbs after long work.

Sleep, rest of things, O pleasing Deity,
Peace of the soul, which cares dost crucify,
Weary bodies refresh and mollify.
   – Ovid

The chiefest thing in all Physick, Paracelsus calls it, above every secret of precious stones and metals. The fittest time is two or three hours after supper, when as the meat is now settled at the bottom of the stomack, and 'tis good to lie on the right side first, because at that site the liver doth rest under the stomack, not molesting any way, but heating him as a fire doth a kettle, that is put to it. After the first sleep 'tis not amiss to lie on the left side, that the meat may the better descend, and sometimes again on the belly, but never on the back. Seven or eight hours is a competent time for a melancholy man to rest, as Crato thinks; but, as some do, to lie in bed and not sleep, a day, or half a day together, to give assent to pleasing conceits and vain imaginations, is many ways pernicious. To procure this sweet moistening sleep, it's best to take away the occasions (if it be possible) that hinder it, and then to use such inward or outward remedies, which may cause it. It is well known, even at this day, (saith Boissardus, in his Tract on magic), that many cannot sleep for Witches and Fascinations, which are too familiar in some places; they call it, giving a person a bad night. But the ordinary causes are heat and dryness, which must first be removed; a hot and dry brain never sleeps well: grief, fears, cares, expectations, anxieties, great businesses, and all violent perturbations of the mind must in some sort be qualified, that you may sleep soundly on either ear, before we can hope for any good repose. He that sleeps in the day time, or is in suspense, fear, any way troubled in mind, or goes to bed upon a full stomack, may never hope for quiet rest in the night; hired lodgings, as the Poet saith, Inns and such like troublesome places are not for sleep; one calls Ostler, another Tapster, one cries and shouts, another sings, whoops, halloos –

Whilst passenger and sailor sing the praise
Of absent love in ancient lays.
– Horace

Who, not accustomed to such noises, can sleep amongst them? he that will intend to take his rest must go to bed with a secure and composed mind, in a quiet place: At night all the world will be lulled to rest: and if that will not serve, or may be not obtained, to seek then such means as are requisite. To lie in clean linen and sweet; before he goes to bed, or in bed, to hear sweet Musick, which Ficinus commends, or as Jobertus, to read some pleasant Author till he be asleep, to have a basin of water still dropping by his bed side, or to lie near that pleasant murmur, of water gliding by with gentle music, some flood-gates, arches, falls of water, like London Bridge, or some continuate noise which may benumb his senses.

A friend's counsel

If then our judgment be so depraved, our reason over-ruled, will precipitated, that we cannot seek our own good, or moderate ourselves, as in this disease commonly it is, the best way for ease is to impart our misery to some friend, not to smother it up in our own breast; canker thrives and flourishes by concealment, etc., and that which was most offensive to us, a cause of fear and grief, another hell; for grief concealed strangles the soul; but when as we shall but impart it to some discreet, trusty, loving friend, it is instantly removed, by his counsel haply, wisdom, persuasion, advice, his good means, which we could not otherwise apply unto ourselves. A friend's counsel is a charm, like mandrake wine, it allayeth our cares; and as a bull that is tied to a fig-tree becomes gentle on a sudden (which some, saith Plutarch, interpret of good words) so is a savage obdurate heart mollified by fair speeches.

Discontents

Yea, but thou thinkest thou art more miserable than the rest, other men are happy in respect of thee, their miseries are but flea-bitings to thine, thou alone art unhappy, none so bad as thyself. Yet if, as Socrates said: all the men in the world should come and bring their grievances together, of body, mind, fortune, sores, ulcers, madness, epilepsies, agues, and all those common calamities of beggary, want, servitude, imprisonment, and lay them on a heap to be equally divided, wouldst thou share alike, and take thy portion, or be as thou art? Without question, thou wouldst be as thou art. – If some Jupiter should say, to give us all content,

Well, be't so then: you, master soldier,
Shall be a merchant; you, sir lawyer,
A country gentleman; go you to this,
That side you; why stand ye? It's well as 'tis.
    – Horace

Every man knows his own, but not others' defects and miseries; and 'tis the nature of all men still to reflect upon themselves, their own misfortunes, not to examine or consider other men's, not to confer themselves with others: to recount their miseries, but not their good gifts, fortunes, benefits, which they have, to ruminate on their adversity, but not once to think on their prosperity, not what they have, but what they want: to look still on them that go before, but not on those infinite numbers that come after. Whereas many a man would think himself in heaven, a petty Prince, if he had but the last part of that fortune which thou so much repinest at, abhorrest, and accountest a most vile and wretched estate. How many thousands want that which thou hast! how many myriads of poor slaves, captives, of such as work day and night in coal-pits, tin-mines, with sore toil to maintain a poor living, of such as labour in body and mind, live in extreme anguish, and pain, all which thou art free from! Thou art most happy if thou couldst be content, and acknowledge thy happiness. We know the value of a thing from the wanting more than from the enjoying; when thou shalt hereafter come to want, that which thou now loathest, abhorrest, and art weary of, and tired with, when 'tis past, thou wilt say thou werest most happy: and, after a little miss, wish with all thine heart thou hadst the same content again, might'st lead but such a life, a world for such a life: the remembrance of it is pleasant. Be silent then, rest satisfied, comfort thyself with other men's misfortunes, and, as the mouldwarp* in Æsop told the fox, complaining for want of a tail, and the rest of his companions: 'You complain of toys, but I am blind, be quiet.' […] No man can have what he will, he may choose whether he will desire that which he hath not: thy lot is fallen, make the best of it. If we should see at all times, (as Endymion is said to have done), who then were happier than his fellow? Our life is but short, a very dream, and, while we look about, eternity is at

* Mole

hand: our life is a pilgrimage on earth, which wise men pass with great alacrity.

Gentility

[W]hat is your Gentry, but, as Hierom saith, riches grown old, ancient wealth? that is the definition of Gentility. The father goes often to the Devil to make his son a Gentleman. For the present, what is it? It began (saith Agrippa) with strong impiety, with tyranny, oppression, etc.; and so it is maintained: wealth began it (no matter how got), wealth continueth and increaseth it. [...] What maintains our Gentry but wealth? Without means, Gentry is naught worth; nothing so contemptible and base: cheaper than seaweed. Saith Nevisanus the lawyer, to dispute of Gentry without wealth, is (saving your reverence) to discuss the original of a mard*. So that it is wealth alone that denominates, money which maintains it, gives being to it, for which every man may have it. And what is their ordinary exercise? *sit to eat, drink, lie down to sleep, and rise to play:* wherein lies their worth and sufficiency? in a few coats of arms, eagles, lions, serpents, bears, tigers, dogs, crosses, bends, fesses and such like baubles, which they commonly set up in their galleries, porches, windows, on bowls, platters, coaches, in tombs, churches, men's sleeves, etc.. If he can hawk and hunt, ride an horse, play at cards and dice, swagger, drink, swear, take tobacco with a grace, sing, dance, wear his clothes in fashion, court and please his mistress, talk big fustian, insult, scorn, strut, contemn others, and use a little mimical and apish compliment above the rest, he is a complete, (O illustrious phrase!) a well-qualified gentleman; these are most of their employments, this their greatest commendation. What is Gentry, this parchment Nobility then, but, as Agrippa defines it, a sanctuary of knavery and naughtiness, a cloke for wickedness and execrable vices, of pride, fraud, contempt, boasting, oppression, dissimulation, lust, gluttony,

* Turd

malice, fornication, adultery, ignorance, impiety? A nobleman therefore, in some likelihood, as he concludes, is an atheist, an oppressor, an epicure, a gull, a dizzard, an illiterate idiot, an outside, a glow-worm, a proud fool, an arrant ass: a slave to his lust and belly, strong only in wantonness.

One sorrow drives out another

'Yea, but I am ashamed, disgraced, dishonoured, degraded, exploded: my notorious crimes and villainies are come to light ('tis bad to be found out), my filthy lust, abominable oppression, and avarice, lies open, my good name's lost, my fortune's gone, I have been stigmatized, whipt at post, arraigned and condemned, I am a common obloquy, I have lost my ears; odious, execrable, abhorred of God and men.' Be content, 'tis but a nine days' wonder, and as one sorrow drives out another, one passion another, one cloud another, one rumour is expelled by another; every day almost come new news unto our ears, as how the Sun was eclipsed, meteors seen i'th' air, monsters born, prodigies, how the Turks were overthrown in Persia, an Earthquake in Helvetia, Calabria, Japan, or China, an inundation in Holland, a great plague in Constantinople, a fire at Prague, a dearth in Germany, such a man is made a Lord, a Bishop, another hanged, deposed, pressed to death, for some murder, treason, rape, theft, oppression, all which we do hear at first with a kind of admiration, detestation, consternation, but by and by they are buried in silence: thy father's dead, thy brother robb'd, wife runs mad, neighbour hath kill'd himself; 'tis heavy, ghastly, fearful news at first, in every man's mouth, table talk; but after a while who speaks or thinks of it? It will be so with thee and thine offence, it will be forgotten in an instant, be it theft, rape, sodomy, murder, incest, treason, etc., thou art not the first offender, nor shalt thou be the last, 'tis no wonder; every hour such malefactors are called in question, nothing so common,

In every nation, under every sky.
  – Juvenal

Comfort thyself, thou art not the sole man. If he that were guiltless himself should fling the first stone at thee, and he alone should accuse thee that were faultless, how many executioners, how many accusers, wouldst thou have! If every man's sins were written in his forehead, and secret thoughts known, how many thousands would parallel, if not exceed, thine offence!

The benefits of wine

Amongst this number of Cordials and Alteratives I do not find a more present remedy than a cup of wine or strong drink, if it be soberly and opportunely used. It makes a man bold, hardy, courageous, whetteth the wit, if moderately taken, (as Plutarch saith), it makes those, which are otherwise dull, to exhale and evaporate like frankincense, or quicken (Xenophon adds) as oil doth fire. A famous cordial Matthiolus calls it, an excellent nutriment to refresh the body, it makes a good colour, a flourishing age, helps concoction, fortifies the stomack, takes away obstructions, provokes urine, drives out excrements, procures sleep, clears the blood, expels wind and cold poisons, attenuates, concocts, dissipates, all thick vapours, and fuliginous humours. And that which is all in all to my purpose, it takes away fear and sorrow.

Bacchus drives away fierce cares.
– Horace

It glads the heart of man; the sweet school of mirth; Helen's bowl, the sole Nectar of the Gods, or that true Nepenthes in Homer, which puts away fear and grief, as Oribasius and some others will, was naught else but a cup of good wine. *It makes the mind of the King and of the fatherless both one, of the bond and free-man, poor and rich; it turneth all his thoughts to joy and mirth, makes him remember no sorrow or debt, but enricheth his heart, and makes him speak by talents.* It gives life itself, spirits, wit, etc.. For which case the Antients called Bacchus, Libur Pater, Releaser, and sacrificed to Bacchus and Pallas still upon an Altar. *Wine measurably drunk, and in time, brings gladness and cheerfulness of mind, it cheereth God and men:* Bacchus, giver of joy, etc.; it makes an old wife dance, and such as are in misery to forget evil, and be merry.

Wine makes a troubled soul to rest,
Though feet with fetters be oppressed.
  – *Tibullus*

Demetrius in Plutarch, when he fell into Seleucus' hands, and was prisoner in Syria, spent his time with dice and drink, that he might so ease his discontented mind, and avoid those continual cogitations of his present condition wherewith he was tormented. Therefore Solomon *bids wine be given to him that is ready to perish, and to him that hath grief of heart; let him drink that he forget his poverty, and remember his misery no more.* It easeth a burdened soul, nothing speedier, nothing better: which the prophet Zachary perceived, when he said, *that in the time of Messias they of Ephraim should be glad, and their heart should rejoice as through wine.* All which makes me very well approve of that pretty description of a feast in Bartholomæus Anglicus, when grace was said, their hands washed, and the Guests sufficiently exhilarated, with good discourse, sweet musick, dainty fare, as a Corollary to conclude the feast, and continue their mirth, a grace cup came in to cheer their hearts, and they drank healths to one another again and again. Which (as J. Fredericus Matensius) was an old custom in all ages in every Commonwealth, so as they be not enforced to drink by coercion, but as in that Royal Feast of Assuerus which lasted 180 days, *without compulsion they drank by order in golden vessels*, when and what they would themselves. This of drink is most easy and parable remedy, a common, a cheap, still ready against fear, sorrow, and such troublesome thoughts, that molest the mind; as brimstone with fire, the spirits on a sudden are enlightened by it. No better Physick (saith Rhasis) for a melancholy man: and he that can keep company, and carouse, needs no other medicines, 'tis enough. His countryman, Avicenna, proceeds further yet, and will have him that is troubled in mind, or melancholy, not to drink only, but now and then to be drunk: excellent good Physick is it for this and many other diseases. Magninus will have them to be so once a month at least, and gives his reasons for it, because it scours the body by vomit, urine, sweat, and all manner of superfluities, and keeps it clean. Of the same mind is Seneca, the Philosopher in his book On Tranquillity, it is good sometimes to be drunk, it helps sorrow, depresseth cares, and so concludes his Tract with a cup of wine: Take, dearest Serenus, what conduces to tranquillity of mind. But these are Epicureal tenents, tending to looseness of life, Luxury and Atheism, maintained alone by some Heathens, dissolute Arabians, profane Christians, and are exploded by Rabbi Moses, Gulielmus Placentius, Valescus de Taranta, and most accurately ventilated by Jo. Sylvaticus, a late writer and Physician of Milan, where you shall find this tenent copiously confuted.

Howsoever you say, if this be true that wine and strong drink have such virtue to expel fear and sorrow, and to exhilarate the mind, ever hereafter let's drink and be merry.

Come, lusty Lydia, fill's a cup of sack,
And, sirrah drawer, bigger pots we lack,
And Scio wines that have so good a smack.
– Horace

I say with him in A. Gellius, let us maintain the vigour of our souls with a moderate cup of wine, (cups made to give gladness, etc.) and drink to refresh our mind; if there be any cold sorrow in it, or torpid bashfulness, let's wash it all away. – Now drown your cares in wine, so saith Horace, so saith Anacreon,

Drink, then, while we may,
For Death is on his way.

Let's drive down care with a cup of wine: and so say I too (though I drink none myself).

The Third Partition

Burton concludes with a close examination of melancholy arising from love and religion.

Love melancholy: preamble

There will not be wanting, I presume, one or other that will much discommend some part of this Treatise of Love-Melancholy, and object (which Erasmus in his preface to Sir Thomas More suspects of his) that it is too light for a Divine, too Comical a subject, to speak of Love-Symptoms, too phantastical, and fit alone for a wanton Poet, a feeling young love-sick gallant, an effeminate Courtier, or some such idle person. And 'tis true they say: for by the naughtiness of men it is so come to pass, as Caussinus observes, that the very name of Love is odious to chaster ears. And therefore some again out of an affected gravity, will dislike all for the name's sake before they read a word; dissembling with him in Petronius, and seem to be angry that their ears are violated with such obscene speeches, that so they may be admired for grave Philosophers, and staid carriage. They cannot abide to hear talk of Love-toys, or amorous discourses; in mien and gesture, what strikes the eye, in their outward actions averse; and yet in their cogitations they are all out as bad, if not worse than others.[...] But let these cavillers and counterfeit Catos know that, as the Lord John answered the Queen in that Italian Guazzo, an old, a grave, discreet man is fittest to discourse of Love matters, because he hath likely more experience, observed more, hath a more staid judgement, can better discern, resolve, discuss, advise, give better cautions and more solid precepts, better inform his auditors in such a subject, and by reason of his riper years sooner divert. Besides, there is nothing here to be excepted at; Love is a species of melancholy, and a necessary part of this my Treatise, which I may not omit. [...] After a harsh and unpleasing discourse of Melancholy, which hath hitherto molested your patience, and tired the author, give him leave with Godfridus the lawyer and Laurentius to recreate himself in this kind after his laborious studies, since so many grave Divines and worthy men have without offence to manners, to help themselves and others, voluntarily written of it.

We are all mad

This that I write depends much on the opinion and authority of others; nor perchance am I mad myself, I only following the steps of those that are. Yet I may be a little off; we have all been mad at one time or another; you yourself, I think, are touched, and this man, and that man, so I must be, too.

Love's effects

Naughty Love, to what dost thou not compel our mortal hearts? How it tickles the hearts of mortal men, I am almost afraid to relate, amazed, and ashamed, it hath wrought such stupend and prodigious effects, such foul offences. Love indeed (I may not deny) first united provinces, built Cities, and by a perpetual generation makes and preserves mankind, propagates the Church; but if it rage, it is no more Love, but burning Lust, a Disease, Phrensy, Madness, Hell. 'Tis death, 'tis an immedicable calamity, 'tis a raging madness; 'tis no virtuous habit this, but a vehement perturbation of the mind, a monster of nature, wit, and art; as Alexis in Athenaeus sets it out, manfully rash, woman-ishly timid, furiously headlong, bitter sweet, a caressing blow, etc..

Bestiality and homosexuality

Semiramis with a horse, Pasiphae with a bull, Aristo Ephesius with a she-ass, Fulvius with a mare, others with dogs, goats, etc., from such combinations in ancient days were sprung monsters, Centaurs, Silvanuses, and prodigious sights to affright mankind. And not with brutes only, but men among themselves, which sin is vulgarly called Sodomy; this vice was customary in olden times with the Orientals, the Greeks without question, the Italians, Africans, Asiaticks: Hercules had Hylas, Polycletus, Dion, Pirithous, Abderus and the Phrygian, and 'tis given out by some that Eurystheus even was his minion. Socrates used to frequent the Gymnasium because of the beauty of the young-sters, feeding his hungry eyes on that spectacle, wherefore Philebus and Phaedo were corrivals, as Charmides and other Dialogues of Plato sufficiently show; and in truth it was this very Socrates who said of Alcibiades: gladly would I keep silent, and indeed I am averse, he offers too much incentive to wantonness. Theodoretus censures this. Plato himself delighted in Agathon, Xenophon in Clinias, Virgil in Alexis, Anacreaon in Bathyllus. But of the portentous lusts of Nero, Claudius and others of infa-mous memory, assailed by Petronius, Suetonius, and others, exceeding all belief, how much more might be looked for here; but 'tis an ancient ill. Among the Asiaticks, Turks, Italians, the vice is customary to this day; sodomy is [in a manner of speaking] the Diana of the Romans; they make a practice of this every-where among the Turks – sowing seed among the rocks, as the poet saith, ploughing the sands; nor are there lacking complaints of it even in the married state, where an opposite part is used from that which is lawful; nothing a more familiar sin among the Italians, who following Lucianus and Tatius, defend themselves in many writings. Johannes de la Casa, Bishop Beventius, calls it a holy act, the smug rascal, and goes so far as to say that Venus should not otherwise be used. Nothing more common among monks, and priestlings, an inordinate passion even to death and madness. Angelus Politianus, because of the love of boys, laid violent hands on himself. And terrible to say, in our own country, within memory, how much that detestable sin hath raged. For, indeed, in the year 1538, the most prudent King Henry the Eighth, through the venerable Doctors of Laws, Thomas Lee and Richard Layton, inspected the cloisters of cowls and compa-nies of priests and votaries, and found among them so great a number of wenchers, gelded youths, debauchees, catamites, boy-things, pederasts, Sodomites, (as it saith in Bale), Ganymedes, etc., that in every one of them you may be certain of a new Gomorrah. But see, if you please, the catalogue of these things in Bale: girls (he saith) are not able to sleep in their beds because of necromantick Friars. If 'tis thus among monks, votaries, and such-like saintly rascals, what may we not suspect in towns, in palaces? what among nobles, what in cellars, how much nastiness, how much filth! I am silent meanwhile as to the uncleanness of self-defiling monks, scarce to be named.[…] Heliogabalus, saith Lampridius in his life of him, welcomed lust at every gateway of his body. Hostius made a looking-glass and so arranged it as to see his virility falsely magnified to his delight, acting both the man and woman at once, a nastiness and abomination even to speak of. 'Tis plain truth, what Plutarch's Gryllus objects to in Ulysses; moreover, he saith, we have not to this day, in the matter of men with men or women with women, so many sorts of vile actions as among your memorable and famous heroes, as Hercules following beardless comrades, mad for his friends, etc.; you are not able to confine your desires within their natural boundaries, but rather, like overflooding rivers, bring about violence, filthiness, turmoil, and confusion of nature in regard to love.

Lust in age

Of women's unnatural, unsatiable lust, what Country, what Village doth not complain? Mother and daughter sometimes dote on the same man, father and son, master and servant on one woman.

> *What have desire and lust unbridled left*
> *Chaste and inviolate upon the earth?*
>   *– Euripides*

What breach of vows and oaths, fury, dotage, madness, might I reckon up! Yet this is more tolerable in youth, and such as are still in their hot blood; but for an old fool to dote, to see an old lecher, what more odious, what can be more absurd? and yet what so common? Who so furious?

> *Those who love in age,*
> *All the more madly rage.*
> *– Plautus*

Some dote then more than ever they did in their youth. How many decrepit, hoary, harsh, writhen, bursten-bellied, crooked, toothless, bald, blear-eyed, impotent, rotten, old men, shall you see flickering still in every place! One gets him a young wife, another a courtesan, and when he can scarce lift his leg over a sill, and hath one foot already in Charon's boat, when he hath the trembling in his joints, the gout in his feet, a perpetual rheum in his head, a continuate cough, his sight fails him, thick of hearing, his breath stinks, all his moisture is dried up and gone, may not spit from him, a very child again, that cannot dress himself, or cut his own meat, yet he will be dreaming of, and honing after* wenches, what can be more unseemly? Worse it is in women than in men, when she is in her declining years, an old widow, a mother so long since (in Pliny's opinion) she doth very unseemly seek to marry, yet whilst she is so old a crone, a beldam, she can neither see, nor hear, go nor stand, a mere carcass, a witch, and scarce feel; she caterwauls, and must have a stallion, a champion, she must and will marry again, and betroth herself to some young man, that hates to look on her but for her goods, abhors the sight of her, to the prejudice of her good name, her own undoing, grief of friends, and ruin of her children.

Personal preference
A little soft hand, pretty little mouth, small, fine, long fingers, 'tis that which Apollo did admire in Daphne; a straight and slender

---

* Yearning for

body, a small foot, and well proportioned leg, hath an excellent lustre, bearing the body like the foundation of a temple. Clearchus vowed to his friend Amynander, in Aristaenetus, that the most attractive part in his Mistress, to make him love and like her first, was her pretty leg and foot; a soft and white skin, etc., have their peculiar graces, a cloud is not softer, by Pollux, than the surface of her lovely breasts. Though in men these parts are not so much respected; a grim Saracen sometimes, a Pyracmon with naked limbs, a martial hirsute face pleaseth best; a black man is a pearl in a fair woman's eye, and is as acceptable as lame Vulcan was to Venus; for he being a sweaty fuliginous blacksmith, was dearly beloved of her, when fair Apollo, nimble Mercury, were rejected, and the rest of the sweet-fac'd gods forsaken. Many women (as Petronius observes) are hot after dirty ones (as many men are more moved with kitchen-wenches, and a poor market-maid, than all these illustrious Court and City Dames), will sooner dote upon a slave, a servant, a Dirt-dauber, a Blacksmith, a Cook, a Player, if they see his naked legs or brawny arms, like that Huntsman Meleager in Philostratus, though he be all in rags, obscene and dirty, besmeared like a ruddle-man*, a gipsy, or a chimney-sweeper, than upon a Noble Gallant, Nireus, Hephæstion, Alcibiades, or those embroidered Courtiers full of silk and gold. Justine's wife, a Citizen of Rome, fell in love with Pylades, a Player, and was ready to run mad for him, had not Galen himself helped her by chance. Faustina the Empress doted on a Fencer.

Not one of a thousand falls in love, but there is some peculiar part or other which pleaseth most, and inflames him above the rest. A company of young Philosophers on a time fell at variance, which part of a woman was most desirable, and pleased best? some said the forehead, some the teeth, some the eyes, cheeks, lip, neck, chin, etc., the controversy was referred to Lais of Corinth to decide; but she, smiling, said they were a company of

* Dealer in red ochre

fools; for suppose they had her where they wished, what would they first seek? Yet, this notwithstanding, I do easily grant, nor, I think, would any of you contradict me, all parts are attractive, but especially the eyes – sparkling and bright as stars – which are Love's Fowlers; the shoeing-horns, the hooks of Love (as Arandus will) the guides, touchstone, judges, that in a moment cure mad men, and make sound folks mad, the watchmen of the body; what do they not?

Foul mistresses

Every Lover admires his Mistress, though she be very deformed of herself, ill-favoured, wrinkled, pimpled, pale, red, yellow, tanned, tallow-faced, have a swollen Juggler's platter-face, or a thin, lean, chitty-face, have clouds in her face, be crooked, dry, bald, goggle-ey'd, blear-ey'd, or with staring eyes, she look like a squis'd* cat, hold her head still awry, heavy, dull, hollow-eyed, black or yellow about the eyes, or squint-eyed, sparrow-mouthed, Perean hook-nosed, have a sharp Fox nose, a red nose, China flat great nose, snub-nose with wide nostrils, a nose like a promontory, gubber-tushed†, rotten teeth, black, uneven, brown teeth, beetle-browed, a Witch's beard, her breath stink all over the room, her nose drop winter and summer, with a Bavarian poke‡ under her chin, a sharp chin, lave-eared§, with a long crane's neck, which stands awry too, with hanging breasts, her dugs like two double jugs, or else no dugs, in the other extreme, bloody-faln¶ fingers, she have filthy long unpared nails, scabbed hands, or wrists, a tanned skin, a rotten carcass, crooked back, she stoops, is lame, splay-footed, as slender in the middle as a Cow in the waist, gouty legs, her ankles hang over her shoes, her

* Squeezed
† With projecting teeth
‡ Pouch
§ Lop-eared
¶ Chillblained

feet stink, she breeds lice, a mere changeling, a very monster, an auf*, imperfect, her whole complexion savours, an harsh voice, incondite gesture, vile gait, a vast virago, or an ugly Tit, a slug, a fat fustilugs, a truss, a long lean raw-bone, a skeleton, a sneaker, (suppose, as the poet saith, her unseen beauties somewhat better), and to thy judgement looks like a merd in a lanthorn, whom thou couldst not fancy for a world, but hatest, loathest, and wouldest have spit in her face, or blow thy nose in her bosom, the very antidote of love to another man, a dowdy, a slut, a scold, a nasty, rank, rammy, filthy, beastly quean, dishonest peradventure, obscene, base, beggarly, rude, foolish, untaught, peevish, Irus' daughter, Thersites' sister, Grobian's scholar, if he love her once, he admires her for all this, he takes no notice of any such errors, or imperfections of body or mind.

> *Those very things enchant him then,*
> *As upon Agna's nose the wen*
> *Charms poor Balbinus,*
>   *– Horace*

He had rather have her than any woman in the world.

Anaphrodisiacs

Here they make medicines to allay lust, such as putting Camphor on the parts, and carrying it in the breeches (one saith) keeps the pintle flaccid. A noble virgin being sick with this affliction, a Physician prescribed for her, among other things, that she wear on her back for twenty days a thin sheet of lead pierced with many holes; and for the drying up of seed he ordered that she be very sparing of victual, and chew frequently a preparation of coriander, lettuce-seed and vinegar, and so freed her of the malady. Further, they hinder or prevent coitus by a willow-leaf rubbed and drunk, and if frequently used, they cease from it

* Elf

wholly. Topaz is likewise recommended, worn in a ring; the right stone of a wolf, brayed; and oil or water of roses will cause weariness of venery, writes Alexander Benedictus; buttermilk, Canabis seed, and Camphor are also commended. Carrying a Verbena herb extinguisheth lust, and pulverized frog, beheaded and dried up. To extinguish coitus, anoint the genitals and belly and chest with water in which opium Thebaicum has been dissolved; Camphor is in the highest degree inimical to lust, and dried coriander diminishes coitus and hinders erection; mustard drink does the same. Give verbena in a potion, and the pintle will not lift for six days; dried mint with vinegar in the uterus, the genitals smeared with juice of Henbane or Hemlock, quiets the appetite for coitus, etc..

Love's best refuge

'Tis an hazard both ways I confess, to live singly, or to marry; it may be bad, it may be good; as it is a cross and calamity on the one side, so 'tis a sweet delight, in incomparable happiness, a blessed estate, a most unspeakable benefit, a sole content on the other; 'tis all in the proof. Be then not so wayward, so covetous, so distrustful, so curious and nice, but let's all marry, lie in mutual warm embrace. Take me to thee, and thee to me, to morrow is St. Valentine's day, let's keep it Holiday for Cupid's sake, for that great God Love's sake, for Hymen's sake, and celebrate Venus' Vigil with our Ancestors for company together, singing as they did,

> *Tomorrow let him love who ne'er loved yet,*
> *Nor let him who e'er loved before forget,*
> *'Tis tuneful spring, the world's new-born in spring*
> *It is love's season, birds then pairing sing,*
> *'Tis then the woods renew their annual green.*
>   *– Pervigilium Veneris*

[...] Since then this of marriage is the last and best refuge and cure of Heroical love, all doubts are cleared, and impediments removed; I say again, what remains, but that according to both their desires, they be happily joined, since it cannot otherwise be helped. God send us all good wives, every man his wish in this kind, and me mine!

Jealousy

Of all passions, as I have already proved, Love is most violent, and of those bitter potions which this Love Melancholy affords, this bastard Jealousy is the greatest, as appears by those prodigious Symptoms which it hath, and that it produceth. For besides Fear and Sorrow, which is common to all Melancholy, anxiety of mind, suspicion, aggravation, restless thoughts, paleness, meagreness, neglect of business, and the like, these men are farther yet misaffected, and in an higher strain. 'Tis a more vehement passion, a more furious perturbation, a bitter pain, a fire, a pernicious curiosity, a gall corrupting the honey of our life, madness, vertigo, plague, hell, they are more than ordinarily disquieted, they lose the blessing of peace of mind, as Chrysostom observes; and though they be rich, keep sumptuous tables, be nobly allied, yet they are most miserable, they are more than ordinarily discontent, more sad, more than ordinarily suspicious. Jealousy, saith Vives, begets unquietness in the mind night and day: he hunts after every word he hears, every whisper, and amplifies it to himself (as all melancholy men do in other matters) with a most unjust calumny of others, he misinterprets every thing is said or done, most apt to mistake or misconster*, he pries into every corner, follows close, observes to an hair. 'Tis proper to Jealousy so to do,

Pale hag, infernal fury, pleasure's smart,
Envy's observer, prying in every part.
  – Daniel

* Misconstrue

Besides these strange gestures of staring, frowning, grinning, rolling of eyes, menacing, ghastly looks, broken pace, interrupt, precipitate, half-turns. He will sometimes sigh, weep, sob for anger,

Such thunder-storms in sooth pour down their showers,

swear and belie, slander any man, curse, threaten, brawl, scold, fight; and sometimes again flatter, and speak fair, ask forgiveness, kiss and coll, condemn his rashness and folly, vow, protest and swear he will never do so again; and then eftsoons, impatient as he is, rave, roar, and lay about him like a mad man, thump her sides, drag her about perchance, drive her out of doors, send her home, he will be divorced forthwith, she is a whore, etc., by and by with all submiss compliment entreat her fair, and bring her in again, he loves her dearly, she is his sweet, most kind, and loving wife, he will not change, not leave her for a Kingdom; so he continues off and on, as the toy takes him, the object moves him, but most part brawling, fretting, unquiet he is, accusing and suspecting not strangers only, but Brothers and Sisters, Father and Mother, nearest and dearest friends. He thinks with those Italians,

Who doth it not in the family
Is one who doth it never or seldomly.

And through fear conceives unto himself things almost incredible and impossible to be effected. As an Heron when she fishes, still prying on all sides, or as a Cat doth a Mouse, his eye is never off hers; he gloats on him, on her, accurately observing on whom she looks, who looks at her, what she saith, doth, at dinner, at supper, sitting, walking, at home, abroad, he is the same, still inquiring, mandering*, gazing, listening, affrighted

* Crying for

93

with every small object; why did she smile, why did she pity him, commend him? why did she drink twice to such a man? why did she offer to kiss, dance? etc., a whore, a whore, an arrant whore! All this he confesseth in the Poet,

Each thing affrights me, I do fear,
Ah pardon me my fear,
I doubt a man is hid within
The clothes that thou dost wear.
  – Propertius

Is't not a man in woman's apparel? is not somebody in that great chest, or behind the door, or hangings, or in some of those barrels? May not a man steal in at the window with a ladder of ropes, or come down the chimney, have a false key, or get in when he is asleep? If a Mouse do but stir, or the wind blow, a casement clatter, that's the villain, there he is; by his good will no man shall see her, salute her, speak with her, she shall not go forth of his sight, so much as to do her needs. Argus did not so keep his Cow, that watchful Dragon the Golden fleece, or Cerberus the coming in of Hell as he keeps his wife. [...] See but with what rigour those jealous husbands tyrannize over their poor wives. In Greece, Spain, Italy, Turkey, Africa, Asia, and generally over all those hot countries, your women are your land, to be ploughed at your will; Mahomet in his Alcoran gives this power to men; your wives are as your land, till them, use them, intreat them fair or foul, as you will yourselves.

I' faith, women live under hard conditions,
  – Plautus

they lock them still in their houses, which are as so many prisons to them, will suffer nobody to come to them, or their wives to be seen abroad. They must not so much as look out. And if they be great persons, they have Eunuchs to keep them, as the Grand

Seignior among the Turks, the Sophies of Persia, those Tartarian Mogors, and Kings of China. Saith Riccius, they geld innumerable infants to this purpose; the King of China maintains 10,000 Eunuchs in his family to keep his wives. The Xeriffes of Barbary keep their Courtesans in such strict manner, that if any man come but in sight of them, he dies for it; and if they chance to see a man, and do not instantly cry out, though from their windows, they must be put to death. The Turks have I know not how many black deformed Eunuchs (for the white serve for other ministeries) to this purpose sent commonly from Egypt, deprived in their childhood of all their privities, and brought up in the Seraglio at Constantinople, to keep their wives; which are so penned up they may not confer with any living man, or converse with younger women, have a Cucumber or Carrot sent in to them for their diet, but sliced, for fear, – etc., and so live, and are left alone to their unchaste thoughts all the days of their lives.

Religious melancholy: preamble

That there is such a distinct species of Love-Melancholy, no man hath ever yet doubted; but whether this subdivision of Religious Melancholy be warrantable, it may be controverted.

> *Lead on, ye Muses, nor desert me now*
> *Mid-journey, where no footsteps go before,*
> *Nor wheel-tracks marking out a way for me.*
>   *– Grotius*

I have no pattern to follow, as in some of the rest, no man to imitate. No Physician hath as yet distinctly written of it, as of the other; all acknowledge it a most notable symptom, but few a species or kind.[…] [A]ll the world again cannot afford so much matter of madness, so many stupid symptoms, as superstition, heresy, schism hath brought out: that this species alone may be parallel'd to all the former, hath greater latitude, and more miraculous effects; that it more besots and infatuates men, than any other above named whatsoever, doth more harm, works more disquietness to mankind, and hath more crucified the souls of mortal men (such hath been the Devil's craft) than wars, plagues, sicknesses, dearth, famine, and all the rest.

Give me but a little leave, and I will set before your eyes in brief a stupend, vast, infinite Ocean of incredible madness and folly: a Sea full of shelves and rocks, sands, gulfs, Euripuses, and contrary tides, full of fearful monsters, uncouth shapes, roaring waves, tempests, and Siren calms, Halcyonian Seas, unspeakable misery, such Comedies and Tragedies, such absurd and ridiculous, feral and lamentable fits, that I know not whether they are more to be pitied or derided, or may be believed, but that we daily see the same still practised in our days, fresh examples, new news, fresh objects of misery and madness in this kind, that are still represented to us, abroad, at home, in the midst of us, in our bosoms.

The Devil's instruments

We are taught in holy Scripture, that *the Devil rangeth abroad like a roaring Lion, still seeking whom he may devour*: and as in several shapes, so by several engines and devices, he goeth about to seduce us; sometimes he transforms himself into an Angel of Light; and is so cunning, that he is able, if it were possible, to deceive the very Elect. [...] His ordinary instruments or factors which he useth, as God himself did good Kings, Lawful Magistrates, patriarchs, prophets, to the establishing of his Church, are Politicians, Statesmen, Priests, Hereticks, blind guides, Impostors, pseudo-Prophets, to propagate his superstition. And first to begin with Politicians, it hath ever been a principal axiom with them, to maintain religion, or superstition, which they determine of, alter and vary upon all occasions, as to them seems best, they make Religion mere policy, a cloak, a human invention; to rule the vulgar with, as Tacitus and Tully hold. Austin censures Scaevola saying and acknowledging, that it was a fit thing cities should be deceived by religion, according to the diverb, If the world will be gulled, let it be gulled, 'tis good howsoever to keep it in subjection. 'Tis that which our late Politicians ingeminate*; Cromerus, Boterus, Clamarius, Arneseus, Captain Machiavel will have a prince by all means to counterfeit religion, to be superstitious in shew at least, to seem to be devout, frequent holy exercises, honour divines, love the Church, affect priests, as Numa, Lycurgus, and such law-makers were, and did, not that they had faith, but that it was an easy way to keep power, to keep people in obedience. [...] Many Politicians, I dare not deny, maintain Religion as a true means, and sincerely speak of it without hypocrisy, are truly zealous and religious themselves. Justice and Religion are the two chief props and supporters of a well-governed commonwealth; but most of them are but Machiavellians, counterfeits only for political ends; for kingship only (which Campanella in his Triumph of Atheism observes), as amongst our modern Turks, as knowing the greatest dominion is that over men's minds; and that as Sabellicus delivers, A man without Religion is like a horse without a bridle. No better way to curb than superstition, to terrify men's consciences, and to keep them in awe: they make new laws, statutes, invent new religions, ceremonies, as so many stalking-horses, to their own ends. If a religion be false, only let it supposed to be true, and it will tame fierce minds, restrain desires, and make loyal subjects.[...] Those French and British Druids in the West first taught, saith Caesar, that souls did not die, but after death went from one to another, that so they might encourage them to virtue. 'Twas for a politick end, and to this purpose the old Poets feigned those Elysian fields, their Aecus, Minos, and Rhadamanthus, their infernal Judges, and those Stygian lakes, fiery Phlegethons, Pluto's Kingdom, and variety of torments after death. Those that had done well went to the Elysian fields, but evil-doers to Cocytus, and to that burning

* Reiterate

lake of Hell, with fire and brimstone for ever to be tormented. 'Tis this which Plato labours for in his Phaedo, and in the third book of his Republick. The Turks in their Alcoran, when they set down rewards and several punishments for every particular virtue and vice, when they persuade men, that they that die in battle shall go directly to Heaven, but wicked livers to eternal torment, and all of all sorts (much like our Papistical Purgatory), for a set time shall be tortured in their graves. […] After a man's death two black Angels, Nunquir and Nequir (so they call them) come to him in his grave and punish him for his precedent sins; if he lived well, they torture him the less; if ill, they incessantly punish him to the day of judgment. The thought of this crucifies them all their lives long, and makes them spend their days in fasting and prayer, lest these evils should come to pass. […] What have they not made the common people believe? Impossibilities in nature, incredible things; what devices, traditions, ceremonies, have they not invented in all ages to keep men in obedience, to enrich themselves? For their enrichment have men's minds been overcome with superstition, as Livy saith. […] [A]bove all others. that High Priest of Rome, the dam of that monstrous and superstitious brood, the bull-bellowing Pope, which now rageth in the West, that three-headed Cerberus, hath played his part. Whose religion at this day is mere policy, a state wholly composed of superstition and wit, and needs nothing but wit and superstition to maintain it, that useth Colleges and religious houses to as good purpose as Forts and Castles, and doth more at this day by a company of scribbling Parasites, fiery-spirited Friars, Zealous Anchorites, hypocritical Confessors, and those Praetorian soldiers, his Janissary Jesuits, that dissociable society, as Langius calls it, the last effort of the Devil and the very excrement of time, that now stand in the forefront of the battle, will have a monopoly of, and engross all other learning, but domineer in Divinity, and fight alone almost (for the rest are but his dromedaries and asses), than ever he could have done by garrisons and armies.

Ignorance and superstition

And the best means they have to broach first or to maintain it when they have done, is to keep them still in ignorance: for Ignorance is the mother of Devotion, as all the world knows, and these times can amply witness. This hath been the Devil's practice, and his infernal Ministers in all ages; not as our Saviour, by a few silly fishermen, to confound the wisdom of the world, to save Publicans and Sinners, but to make advantage of their ignorance, to convert them and their associates, and that they may better effect what they intend, they begin, as I say, with poor, stupid, illiterate persons. So Mahomet did when he published his Alcoran, which is a piece of work (saith Bredenbachius) full of nonsense, barbarism, confusion without rhyme, reason, or any good composition, first published to a company of rude rusticks, hog-rubbers, that had no discretion, judgment, art, or understanding, and is so still maintained. For it is a part of their policy to let no man comment, dare to dispute or call in question to this day any part of it, be it never so absurd, incredible, ridiculous, fabulous as it is, it must be believed implicitly upon pain of death, no man must dare to contradict it, God and Emperor etc.. What else do our Papists but, by keeping the people in ignorance, vent and broach all their new ceremonies and traditions, when they conceal the Scripture, read it in Latin, and to some few alone, feeding the slavish people in the mean time with tales out of Legends, and such like fabulous narrations? Whom do they begin with but collapsed Ladies, some few tradesmen, superstitious old folks, illiterate persons, weak women, discontent, rude, silly companions, or sooner circumvent? So do all our schismaticks and hereticks.

Sectarian hatred

What Religion is, and of what parts it doth consist, every Catechism will tell you, what Symptoms it hath, and what effects it produceth: but for their superstitions, no tongue can tell them, no pen express, they are so many, so diverse, so uncertain, so unconstant, and so different from themselves. [...] Of these symptoms some be general, some particular to each private sect: general to all, are, an extraordinary love and affection they bear and shew to such as are of their own sect, and more than Vatinian hate to such as are opposite in Religion, as they call it, or disagree from them in their superstitious rites, blind zeal, (which is as much a symptom as a cause), vain fears, blind obedience, needless works, incredibilities, impossibilities, monstrous rites and ceremonies, wilfulness, blindness, obstinacy, etc.. For the first, which is love and hate, as Montanus saith, no greater concord, no greater discord than that which proceeds from Religion. It is incredible to relate, did not our daily experience evince it, what factions, (as Rich. Dinoth writes), have been of late for matters of Religion in France, and what hurly burlies all over Europe for these many years. [...] [W]e read of bloody battles, racks and wheels, seditions, factions, oppositions, standards facing standards, eagles matching eagles, and spear threatening spear, invectives and contentions. They had rather shake hands with a Jew, Turk, or as the Spaniards do, suffer Moors to live amongst them, and Jews, than Protestants; my name (saith Luther) is more odious to them than any thief or murderer. So it is with all hereticks and schismaticks whatsoever: and none so passionate, violent in their tenents, opinions, obstinate, wilful, refractory, peevish, factious, singular and stiff in defence of them; they do not only persecute and hate, but pity all other Religions, account them damned, blind, as if they alone were the true Church, they are the true heirs, have the fee simple* of heaven by a peculiar donation, 'tis entailed on them and their posterities, their doctrine sound, they alone are to be saved.

Islam

Mahometans are a compound of Gentiles, Jews, and Christians, and so absurd in their ceremonies, as if they had taken that

* Freehold

which is most sottish out of every one of them, full of idle fables in their superstitious law, their Alcoran itself a gallimaufry of lies, tales, ceremonies, traditions, precepts, stole from other sects, and confusedly heaped up to delude a company of rude and barbarous clowns. As how birds, beasts, stones, saluted Mahomet when he came from Mecca, the Moon came down from heaven to visit him, how God sent for him, spake to him, etc., with a company of stupend figures of the Angels, Sun, Moon, and Stars, etc.. Of the day of judgement, and three sounds to prepare to it, which must last 50,000 years, of Paradise, which wholly consists in wenching and feasting, and what is written about flocks [for provender], herds in Paradise, is so ridiculous, that Virgil, Dante, Lucian, nor any Poet can be more fabulous. Their Rites and Ceremonies are most vain and superstitious, Wine and Swine's-flesh are utterly forbidden by their Law, they must pray five times a day, and still towards the South; wash before and after all their bodies over, with many such. For fasting, vows, religious orders, peregrinations, they go far beyond any Papists, they fast together a month together many times, and must not eat a bit till Sun be set. Their Kalenders, Dervises, and Torlachers* etc., are more abstemious some of them, than Carthusians, Franciscans, Anachorites, forsake all, live solitary, fare hard, go naked, etc.. [...] [They] go as far as Mahomet's Tomb, which journey is both miraculous and meritorious. The ceremonies of flinging stones to stone the Devil, of eating a Camel at Cairo by the way; their fastings, their running till they sweat, their long prayers, Mahomet's Temple, Tomb, and building of it, would ask a whole volume to dilate; and for their pains taken in this holy Pilgrimage, all their sins are forgiven, and they reputed for so many Saints. [...] Many foolish Ceremonies you shall find in them; and which is most to be lamented, the people are generally so curious in observing of them, that if the least Circumstance be

* Mendicants

omitted, they think they shall be damned, 'tis an irremissible offence, and can hardly be forgiven. I kept in my house amongst my followers (saith Busbequius, sometime the Turk's Orator in Constantinople) a Turkey boy, that by chance did eat shell-fish, a meat forbidden by their Law, but the next day when he knew what he had done, he was not only sick to cast and vomit, but very much troubled in mind, would weep and grieve many days after, torment himself for his foul offence. Another Turk, being to drink a cup of wine in his Cellar, first made a huge noise, and filthy faces, to warn his soul, as he said, that it should not be guilty of that foul fact which he was to commit. With such toys as these are men kept in awe, and so cowed, that they dare not resist, or offend the least circumstance of their Law, for conscience sake, misled by superstition, which no human edict otherwise, no force of arms, could have enforced.

Latter-day prophets

We are never likely seven years together without some such new Prophets, that have several inspirations, some to convert the Jews, some fast forty days, go with Daniel to the Lion's den; some foretell strange things, some for one thing, some for another. Great Precisians of mean conditions and very illiterate, most part by preposterous zeal, fasting, meditation, melancholy, are brought into these gross errors and inconveniences. Of these men I may conclude generally, that howsoever they may seem to be discreet, and men of understanding in other matters, discourse well, they have a diseased imagination, they are like comets, round in all places but only where they blaze, otherwise sane, they have impregnable wits many of them, and discreet otherwise, but in this their madness and folly breaks out beyond measure. They are certainly far gone with melancholy, if not quite mad, and have more need of physic than many a man that keeps his bed, more need of Hellebore than those that are in Bedlam.

Despair

As shoe-makers do when they bring home shoes, still cry, Leather is dearer and dearer; may I justly say of those melancholy Symptoms, these of Despair are most violent, tragical and grievous, far beyond the rest, not to be expressed, but negatively, as it is privation of all happiness, not to be endured; *for a wounded spirit who can bear?* What therefore Timanthes did in his picture of Iphigenia, now ready to be sacrificed, when he had painted Calchas mourning, Ulysses sad, but most sorrowful Menelaus, and shewed all his art in expressing variety of affections, he covered the maid's father, Agamemnon's head, with a veil, and left it to every spectator to conceive what he would himself; for that true passion and sorrow in the highest degree, such as his was, could not by any art be deciphered. What he did in his picture, I will do in describing the Symptoms of Despair; imagine what thou canst, fear, sorrow, furies, grief, pain, terror, anger, dismal, ghastly, tedious, irksome, etc., it is not sufficient, it comes far short, no tongue can tell, no heart conceive it. 'Tis an Epitome of hell, an extract, a quintessence, a compound, a mixture of all feral maladies, tyrannical tortures, plagues and perplexities. There is no sickness, almost, but Physick provideth a remedy for it; to every sore Chirurgery will provide a salve: friendship helps poverty; hope of liberty easeth imprisonment; suit and favour revoke banishment; authority and time wear away reproach: but what Physick, what Chirurgery, what wealth, favour, authority can relieve, bear out, assuage, or expel a troubled conscience? A quiet mind cureth all them, but all they cannot comfort a distressed soul: who can put to silence the voice of desperation? All that is single in other melancholy, horrible, dire, pestilent, cruel, relentless, concur in this, it is more than melancholy in the highest degree; a burning fever of the soul; so mad, saith Jacchinus, by this misery; fear, sorrow, and despair he puts for ordinary symptoms of Melancholy. They are in great pain and horror of mind, distraction of soul, restless, full of continual fears, cares, torments, anxieties, they can neither eat, drink, nor sleep for them, take no rest,

Neither at bed nor yet at board,
Will any rest despair afford.
  – Juvenal

Fear takes away their content, and dries the blood, wasteth the marrow, alters their countenance, even in their greatest delights, singing, dancing, dalliance, they are still (saith Lemnius) tortured in their souls.

Overcoming despair

Experience teacheth us, that though many die obstinate and wilful in this malady, yet multitudes again are able to resist and overcome, seek for help, and find comfort, are taken from the chops of Hell, and out of the Devil's paws, though they have by obligation given themselves to him. Some out of their own strength, and God's assistance, *though he kill me* (saith Job) *yet will I trust in him*, out of good counsel, advice, and Physick. Bellovacus cured a Monk, by altering his habit, and course of life: Plater many by Physick alone. But for the most part they must concur: and they take a wrong course, that think to overcome this feral passion by sole Physick; and they are as much out, that think to work this effect by good advice alone, though both be forcible in themselves, yet they must go hand in hand to this disease:

Each requires the others' aid.
  – Horace

For Physick, the like course is to be taken with this, as in other Melancholy: diet, air, exercise, all those passions and perturbations of the mind, etc., are to be rectified by the same means. They must not be left solitary, or to themselves, never idle, never out of company. Counsel, good comfort is to be applied, as they shall see the parties inclined, or to the causes, whether it be loss, fear, grief, discontent, or some such feral accident, a guilty conscience, or otherwise by frequent meditation, too grievous an apprehension, and consideration of his former life; by hearing, reading of Scriptures, good Divines, good advice and conference, applying God's Word to their distressed souls, it must be corrected and counter-poised.

Valediction
Only take this for a corollary and conclusion, as thou tenderest thine own welfare in this, and all other melancholy, thy good health of body and mind, observe this short Precept, give not way to solitariness and idleness. Be not solitary, be not idle.

Biographical note

Robert Burton was born in 1577 into a gentry family at Lindley Hall, near Nuneaton in Leicestershire. He attended the local grammar schools at Sutton Coldfield and Nuneaton and followed his elder brother William, the antiquary and historian of Leicestershire, to Brasenose College, Oxford, in 1593. Between 1593 and 1599 he disappears from official records. In 1599 he was admitted as student, or fellow, of Christ Church, Oxford.

He remained at Christ Church for the rest of his life. He was given the living of St Thomas's, on the outskirts of Oxford, in 1616 and practised as a vicar there. In 1624, he was presented with the living of Walesby in Lincolnshire, which he gave up in 1631. The next year he was given (by the Berkeley family) the more lucrative benefice of Seagrave in Leicestershire. In 1615, 1617 and 1618, he was a clerk of Oxford market and from 1624 until his death, librarian of Christ Church. He contributed verse to various poetry collections and wrote part of a play, *Alba*, performed before James I in 1605. He wrote a second play, *Philosophaster*, which was performed in 1618.

He published the first edition of his great work, *The Anatomy of Melancholy*, in 1621. It was a popular success and he added thousands of words to each of the five subsequent editions which appeared in his lifetime. He was himself, as his *Anatomy* suggests, afflicted by melancholy, but not defeated by it. According to Anthony Wood, 'as he was by many accounted a severe student, a devourer of authors, a melancholy and humorous [temperamental] person; so by others, who knew him well, a person of great honesty, plain dealing and charity. I have heard some of the antients of Ch[rist] Ch[urch] often say that his company was very merry, facete and juvenile [or amusing and lively].' This seems to be supported by the engaging portrait of Burton which hangs at Brasenose, which shows a soberly dressed scholar with an open book before him, wearing an amused smile.

He died in 1640, having, as his epitaph in the Cathedral at Christ Church declares, 'devoted his life and death to melancholy'.

Nicholas Robins works for Shakespeare's Globe, where he edits its publications, including the magazine *Around the Globe*. He has written a book on Shakespeare's London and co-edited the *Oxford Guide to Literary Britain and Ireland* (with Daniel Hahn). In 2011, his *John Donne* was published in the Poetic Lives series by Hesperus. He has been a regular contributor to the *London Magazine* and the *Times Literary Supplement*.

He lives in London and Dorset.

Under our three imprints, Hesperus Press publishes over 300 books by many of the greatest figures in worldwide literary history, as well as contemporary and debut authors well worth discovering.

Hesperus Classics handpicks the best of worldwide and translated literature, introducing forgotten and neglected books to new generations.

Hesperus Nova showcases quality contemporary fiction and non-fiction designed to entertain and inspire.

Hesperus Minor rediscovers well-loved children's books from the past – these are books which will bring back fond memories for adults, which they will want to share with their children and loved ones.

To find out more visit www.hesperuspress.com
@HesperusPress

SELECTED TITLES FROM HESPERUS PRESS

Author	Title	Foreword writer
Pietro Aretino	*The School of Whoredom*	Paul Bailey
Pietro Aretino	*The Secret Life of Nuns*	
Jane Austen	*Lesley Castle*	Zoë Heller
Jane Austen	*Love and Friendship*	Fay Weldon
Honoré de Balzac	*Colonel Chabert*	A.N. Wilson
Charles Baudelaire	*On Wine and Hashish*	Margaret Drabble
Giovanni Boccaccio	*Life of Dante*	A.N. Wilson
Charlotte Brontë	*The Spell*	
Emily Brontë	*Poems of Solitude*	Helen Dunmore
Mikhail Bulgakov	*Fatal Eggs*	Doris Lessing
Mikhail Bulgakov	*The Heart of a Dog*	A.S. Byatt
Giacomo Casanova	*The Duel*	Tim Parks
Miguel de Cervantes	*The Dialogue of the Dogs*	Ben Okri
Geoffrey Chaucer	*The Parliament of Birds*	
Anton Chekhov	*The Story of a Nobody*	Louis de Bernières
Anton Chekhov	*Three Years*	William Fiennes
Wilkie Collins	*The Frozen Deep*	
Joseph Conrad	*Heart of Darkness*	A.N. Wilson
Joseph Conrad	*The Return*	Colm Tóibín
Gabriele D'Annunzio	*The Book of the Virgins*	Tim Parks
Dante Alighieri	*The Divine Comedy: Inferno*	
Dante Alighieri	*New Life*	Louis de Bernières
Daniel Defoe	*The King of Pirates*	Peter Ackroyd
Marquis de Sade	*Incest*	Janet Street-Porter
Charles Dickens	*The Haunted House*	Peter Ackroyd
Charles Dickens	*A House to Let*	
Fyodor Dostoevsky	The Double	Jeremy Dyson
Fyodor Dostoevsky	Poor People	Charlotte Hobson
Alexandre Dumas	*One Thousand and One Ghosts*	

George Eliot	*Amos Barton*	Matthew Sweet
Henry Fielding	*Jonathan Wild the Great*	Peter Ackroyd
F. Scott Fitzgerald	*The Popular Girl*	Helen Dunmore
Gustave Flaubert	*Memoirs of a Madman*	Germaine Greer
Ugo Foscolo	*Last Letters of Jacopo Ortis*	Valerio Massimo Manfredi
Elizabeth Gaskell	*Lois the Witch*	Jenny Uglow
Théophile Gautier	*The Jinx*	Gilbert Adair
André Gide	*Theseus*	
Johann Wolfgang von Goethe	*The Man of Fifty*	A.S. Byatt
Nikolai Gogol	*The Squabble*	Patrick McCabe
E.T.A. Hoffmann	*Mademoiselle de Scudéri*	Gilbert Adair
Victor Hugo	*The Last Day of a Condemned Man*	Libby Purves
Joris-Karl Huysmans	*With the Flow*	Simon Callow
Henry James	*In the Cage*	Libby Purves
Franz Kafka	*Metamorphosis*	Martin Jarvis
Franz Kafka	*The Trial*	Zadie Smith
John Keats	*Fugitive Poems*	Andrew Motion
Heinrich von Kleist	*The Marquise of O–*	Andrew Miller
Mikhail Lermontov	*A Hero of Our Time*	Doris Lessing
Nikolai Leskov	*Lady Macbeth of Mtsensk*	Gilbert Adair
Carlo Levi	*Words are Stones*	Anita Desai
Xavier de Maistre	*A Journey Around my Room*	Alain de Botton
André Malraux	*The Way of the Kings*	Rachel Seiffert
Katherine Mansfield	*Prelude*	William Boyd
Edgar Lee Masters	*Spoon River Anthology*	Shena Mackay
Guy de Maupassant	*Butterball*	Germaine Greer
Prosper Mérimée	*Carmen*	Philip Pullman
Sir Thomas More	*The History of King Richard III*	Sister Wendy Beckett
Sándor Petőfi	*John the Valiant*	George Szirtes
Francis Petrarch	*My Secret Book*	Germaine Greer

Luigi Pirandello	*Loveless Love*	
Edgar Allan Poe	*Eureka*	Sir Patrick Moore
Alexander Pope	*The Rape of the Lock and A Key to the Lock*	Peter Ackroyd
Antoine-François Prévost	*Manon Lescaut*	Germaine Greer
Marcel Proust	*Pleasures and Days*	A.N. Wilson
Alexander Pushkin	*Dubrovsky*	Patrick Neate
Alexander Pushkin	*Ruslan and Lyudmila*	Colm Tóibín
François Rabelais	*Pantagruel*	Paul Bailey
François Rabelais	*Gargantua*	Paul Bailey
Christina Rossetti	*Commonplace*	Andrew Motion
George Sand	*The Devil's Pool*	Victoria Glendinning
Jean-Paul Sartre	*The Wall*	Justin Cartwright
Friedrich von Schiller	*The Ghost-seer*	Martin Jarvis
Mary Shelley	*Transformation*	
Percy Bysshe Shelley	*Zastrozzi*	Germaine Greer
Stendhal	*Memoirs of an Egotist*	Doris Lessing
Robert Louis Stevenson	*Dr Jekyll and Mr Hyde*	Helen Dunmore
Theodor Storm	*The Lake of the Bees*	Alan Sillitoe
Leo Tolstoy	*The Death of Ivan Ilych*	
Leo Tolstoy	*Hadji Murat*	Colm Tóibín
Ivan Turgenev	*Faust*	Simon Callow
Mark Twain	*The Diary of Adam and Eve*	John Updike
Mark Twain	*Tom Sawyer, Detective*	
Oscar Wilde	*The Portrait of Mr W.H.*	Peter Ackroyd
Virginia Woolf	*Carlyle's House and Other Sketches*	Doris Lessing
Virginia Woolf	*Monday or Tuesday*	Scarlett Thomas
Emile Zola	*For a Night of Love*	A.N. Wilson